Women in the New Testament

Titles in the OneBook Daily-Weekly series

OneBook.

DAILY-WEEKLY

Women in the New Testament

Suzanne Nicholson

 Seedbed

Unless otherwise noted, Scripture quotations are taken from New Revised Standard
Version Bible, copyright © 1989 National Council of the Churches of Christ
in the United States of America. Used by permission. All rights reserved.

Scripture quotations marked NIV are taken from the Holy Bible, New International
Version®, NIV® Copyright © 1973, 1978, 1984, 2011 by Biblica, Inc.™ Used by
permission of Zondervan. All rights reserved worldwide. www.zondervan.com The
"NIV" and "New International Version" are trademarks registered in the United
States Patent and Trademark Office by Biblica, Inc.™ All rights reserved worldwide.

Scripture quotations marked ESV are from the ESV® Bible (The Holy Bible,
English Standard Version®), copyright © 2001 by Crossway, a publishing
ministry of Good News Publishers. Used by permission. All rights reserved.

Printed in the United States of America

Cover design by Strange Last Name
Page design by PerfecType, Nashville, Tennessee

Nicholson, Suzanne.
    Women in the New Testament / Suzanne Nicholson. – Franklin, Tennessee :
Seedbed Publishing, ©2020.

    pages ; cm. + 1 videodisc – (OneBook. Daily-weekly)

    ISBN 9781628247572 (paperback)
    ISBN 9781628247619 (DVD)
    ISBN 9781628247589 (Mobi)
    ISBN 9781628247596 (ePub)
    ISBN 9781628247602 (uPDF)

    1. Women in the Bible. 2. Bible. New Testament--Biography.
    I. Title. II. Series.

BS2445.N52 2020   225.9/22   2020937860

SEEDBED PUBLISHING
Franklin, Tennessee
seedbed.com

CONTENTS

Contents

Contents

Week Eight
Trajectories of Restoration   **87**

WELCOME TO ONEBOOK DAILY-WEEKLY

John Wesley, in a letter to one of his leaders, penned the following:

> O begin! Fix some part of every day for private exercises. You may acquire
> the taste which you have not: what is tedious at first, will afterwards be
> pleasant. Whether you like it or not, read and pray daily. It is for your life;
> there is no other way; else you will be a trifler all your days. . . . Do justice
> to your own soul; give it time and means to grow. Do not starve yourself
> any longer. Take up your cross and be a Christian altogether.

Rarely are our lives most shaped by our biggest ambitions and highest
aspirations. Rather, our lives are most shaped, for better or for worse, by those
small things we do every single day.

At Seedbed, our biggest ambition and highest aspiration is to resource the
followers of Jesus to become lovers and doers of the Word of God every single
day, to become people of One Book.

To that end, we have created the OneBook Daily-Weekly. First, it's important to understand what this is not: warm, fuzzy, sentimental devotions. If you
engage the Daily-Weekly for any length of time, you will learn the Word of
God. You will grow profoundly in your love for God, and you will become a
passionate lover of people.

How Does the Daily-Weekly Work?

Daily. As the name implies, every day invites a short but substantive engagement with the Bible. Five days a week you will read a passage of Scripture
followed by a short segment of teaching and closing with questions for reflec-
tion and self-examination. On the sixth day, you will review and reflect on the
previous five days.

Weekly. Each week, on the seventh day, find a way to gather with at least
one other person doing the study. Pursue the weekly guidance for gathering.
Share learning, insight, encouragement, and most important, how the Holy
Spirit is working in your lives.

That's it. Depending on the length of the study, when the eight or twelve weeks are done, we will be ready with the next study. On an ongoing basis, we will release new editions of the Daily-Weekly. Over time, those who pursue this course of learning will develop a rich library of Bible learning resources for the long haul.

OneBook Daily-Weekly will develop eight- and twelve-week studies that cover the entire Old and New Testaments. Seedbed will publish new studies regularly so that an ongoing supply of group lessons will be available. All titles will remain accessible, which means they can be used in any order that fits your needs or the needs of your group.

If you are looking for a substantive study to learn Scripture through a steadfast method, look no further.

WEEK ONE

Women at the Beginning

ONE

Elizabeth

Luke 1:5–7, 24–25, 39–45 ESV *In the days of Herod, king of Judea, there was a priest named Zechariah, of the division of Abijah. And he had a wife from the daughters of Aaron, and her name was Elizabeth. ⁶And they were both righteous before God, walking blamelessly in all the commandments and statutes of the Lord. ⁷But they had no child, because Elizabeth was barren, and both were advanced in years. . . .*

²⁴After these days his wife Elizabeth conceived, and for five months she kept herself hidden, saying, ²⁵"Thus the Lord has done for me in the days when he looked on me, to take away my reproach among people." . . .

³⁹In those days Mary arose and went with haste into the hill country, to a town in Judah, ⁴⁰and she entered the house of Zechariah and greeted Elizabeth. ⁴¹And when Elizabeth heard the greeting of Mary, the baby leaped in her womb. And Elizabeth was filled with the Holy Spirit, ⁴²and she exclaimed with a loud cry, "Blessed are you among women, and blessed is the fruit of your womb! ⁴³And why is this granted to me that the mother of my Lord should come to me? ⁴⁴For behold, when the sound of your greeting came to my ears, the baby in my womb leaped for joy. ⁴⁵And blessed is she who believed that there would be a fulfillment of what was spoken to her from the Lord."

Read all of Luke 1:5–25, 39–45.

Key Observation. Sometimes faith takes a long time to prove true.

Understanding the Word. Although prophets had preached about the coming of the Messiah for hundreds of years prior to Jesus' birth, women are the first to proclaim the good news that the Christ has arrived. This week we will explore the ways in which God speaks through these faithful women.

Elizabeth is the wife of a priest. She is from a good family—her ancestors were priests too. Nonetheless, Elizabeth faces disgrace because she is barren. She lives in a culture where having children to carry on the family name means everything. If God doesn't bless a family with many babies, people suspect that some hidden sin is the cause. This belief forces Luke to state that both Elizabeth and her husband are blameless (v. 6). Sometimes bad things do happen to good people.

Elizabeth has a second strike against her. She is elderly and has already gone through menopause. Even though she and Zechariah have prayed for children, their years of waiting have proved fruitless. Elizabeth's frustrating situation mirrors that of Israel. The chosen people of God have longed for freedom from the rule of idol-worshipping foreigners. Blessed but barren; favored but conquered.

The personal and national woes begin to find relief when the angel Gabriel speaks to Zechariah during his temple service. Not only will Elizabeth bear a son, but this child will become a great prophet, filled with the same Holy Spirit as the prophets of old. He will prepare the people of Israel for the fulfillment of God's great plan. But the elderly priest of God doubts. Of all people, he should remember the biblical stories about barren women giving birth! In response, Gabriel strikes Zechariah mute. Zechariah's lack of faith is contrasted with the faith of his wife, who remains in seclusion while she reflects on all that God has done for her.

Elizabeth's seclusion is broken when her young relative, Mary, comes to visit. After five months, Elizabeth's pregnancy is now visible and undeniable; it provides a clear sign for Mary that God does indeed create life in impossible places. Gabriel's prophecy that Elizabeth's baby would be filled with the Holy Spirit "even from his mother's womb" (v. 15) has come true; when the baby hears Mary's voice, he begins to jump in Elizabeth's womb. Elizabeth, too, is filled with the Holy Spirit and she prophetically sees that Mary is pregnant and the child will be her Lord. Elizabeth's rejoicing ("blessed is she who believed" in v. 45) points out the ironic contrast between Zechariah and Mary: the young, uneducated girl believes the angel, whereas the experienced priest did not.

One of Luke's themes throughout his Gospel is the reversal of fortune—the weak and lowly are raised up while the rich and powerful are brought low. In a culture where women had little status or honor, Luke begins by describing a doubting man and a faithful woman. He will revisit this theme at the end of his story when faithful women at the empty tomb proclaim to the doubting disciples that Jesus has risen.

1. Which character do you identify with most? Why?

2. How were Elizabeth's prayers met beyond her wildest expectations?

3. What are ways to be encouraged and keep the faith when it seems that God is taking a long time to act?

T W O

Mary: Painful Obedience (Part One)

Luke 1:26–35, 37–38 *In the sixth month the angel Gabriel was sent by God to a town in Galilee called Nazareth, ²⁷to a virgin engaged to a man whose name was Joseph, of the house of David. The virgin's name was Mary. ²⁸And he came to her and said, "Greetings, favored one! The Lord is with you." ²⁹But she was much perplexed by his words and pondered what sort of greeting this might be. ³⁰The angel said to her, "Do not be afraid, Mary, for you have found favor with God. ³¹And now, you will conceive in your womb and bear a son, and you will name him Jesus. ³²He will be great, and will be called the Son of the Most High, and the Lord God will give to him the throne of his ancestor David. ³³He will reign over the house of Jacob forever, and of his kingdom there will be no end." ³⁴Mary said to the angel, "How can this be, since I am a virgin?" ³⁵The angel said to her, "The Holy Spirit will come upon you, and the power of the Most High will overshadow you; therefore the child to be born will be holy; he will be called Son of God. . . . ³⁷For nothing will be impossible with God." ³⁸Then Mary said, "Here am I, the* *servant of the Lord; let it be with me according to your word." Then the angel departed from her.*

Read also Matthew 1:18–25; Luke 1:46–55.

Key Observation. God's calling can be unexpected and even filled with difficulty.

Understanding the Word. Mary is likely twelve or thirteen years old when the angel Gabriel explains God's shocking plan. She is engaged to Joseph, who is a descendant of the great King David. They are not yet married, although the engagement is a legally binding agreement. (This is why some translations of Matthew 1:19 say Joseph planned to divorce her after he learns she is pregnant.) Mary had likely envisioned that her role in life was to get married, have many sons, and faithfully raise them to love and obey the God of Israel. In that order. She never expected to get pregnant first! Gabriel reassures her that the child will fulfill God's promises from long ago that David's kingdom will last forever (see 2 Samuel 7:16; Isaiah 9:6–7).

Mary responds by questioning Gabriel. She clearly interprets Gabriel to mean that she will conceive while remaining a virgin, and yet all of the Old Testament examples of miraculous births involved married women conceiving children with their husbands. Thus, the miracle of Jesus' birth is even greater than the miracle of John's birth. Gabriel's explanation that the Holy Spirit will "overshadow" Mary makes it clear that this will be a spiritual, not sexual, union. Luke is intentionally contrasting this process with the Greco-Roman myths of the day, in which gods descended to the earth in human form and sexually reproduced with human women. Thus, the child born to Mary will be holy, but as with so many things that the God of Israel does, this child will be like nothing ever imagined.

Gabriel encourages Mary by telling her that Elizabeth, too, has been blessed by God to have a child (v. 36). After visiting her and witnessing God's provision, Mary offers a beautiful hymn of praise to God (see 1:46–55). Her song echoes Hannah's song in 1 Samuel 2:1–10 and highlights Luke's theme of reversal of fortunes; God has brought down the wealthy and powerful and lifted up the humble.

Nonetheless, the honor of bearing the Son of God will include great difficulty. When Mary says yes to God's plan, she will be subjecting herself to ridicule and even the threat of death. If Joseph wanted to pursue the full extent of the Law, he could have Mary stoned to death for being unfaithful (see Deuteronomy 22:23–24). This would preserve his honor. Presumably the angel's words to Mary reassure her that this will not happen, since the angel promises the child will grow to be great. Even so, she will experience the shame of being pregnant out of wedlock; her family and neighbors will assume she is an adulteress. Even her relationship with Joseph is strained at first. Matthew's Gospel explains that the righteous Joseph wants to dismiss his fiancée when he finds out she is pregnant. Yet he is compassionate and does not want to publicly shame her. Only after an angel confirms God's plan does Joseph return to Mary (see Matthew 1:18–25). In order to fulfill God's plan, he will face the shame of his wife's rumored adultery.

1. Why do Christians sometimes think God's calling should be easy? How does this passage, as well as other stories in Scripture, correct that viewpoint?

2. Despite the shame Mary had to bear, why did she rejoice?

3. God's calling upon Mary's life provided both blessing and hardship. Describe ways that God's calling in your own life has reflected this same dynamic.

THREE

Anna

Luke 2:22–24, 36–38 NIV *When the time came for the purification rites required by the Law of Moses, Joseph and Mary took him to Jerusalem to present him to the Lord* [23](*as it is written in the Law of the Lord, "Every firstborn male is to be consecrated to the Lord"*), [24]*and to offer a sacrifice in keeping with what is said in the Law of the Lord: "a pair of doves or two young pigeons."* . . .

[36]*There was also a prophet, Anna, the daughter of Penuel, of the tribe of Asher. She was very old; she had lived with her husband seven years after her*

marriage, ³⁷and then was a widow until she was eighty-four. She never left the temple but worshiped night and day, fasting and praying. ³⁸Coming up to them at that very moment, she gave thanks to God and spoke about the child to all who were looking forward to the redemption of Jerusalem.

Read all of Luke 2:22–38.

Key Observation. A posture of prayer often leads to revelation.

Understanding the Word. When this story begins, Mary and Joseph are faithfully observing Jewish laws. The couple had Jesus circumcised on the eighth day as required by the Law, and they named him Jesus, just as the angel had instructed them (2:21). Now they have traveled from Bethlehem to Jerusalem so they can perform the temple rituals required by the Law: the consecration of the firstborn (see Exodus 13:2, 15) and the purification sacrifice (see Leviticus 12:1–8). The couple offers two doves, which is the sacrifice the poor are allowed to make instead of the more expensive lamb. Luke thus shows that the Savior of the world—the King of kings and Lord of lords—is born into a lower-class family. This and other details of the birth narrative (such as the angelic birth announcement made to blue-collar shepherds) present the gospel as accessible to all people.

As Luke often does in his Gospel, he now presents a male-female pairing in his story. Simeon and Anna both announce the redemption of Israel. Both are elderly. Simeon has been promised that he will not die until he sees the Messiah. Although we are not told his age, once he has seen Jesus, he is ready to die in peace (vv. 26, 29). Anna is at least 84 years old, although the Greek could mean that she was a widow for eighty-four years. If she was 12 to 14 when married and then widowed after seven years, she could be as old as 105. In either case, she has been spending decades in the temple courts, regularly praying and fasting. When her routine changes on this day, people will notice.

Simeon and Anna together also represent the whole of Israel. Anna is from the northern tribe of Asher. Although the northern tribes had been dispersed during the Assyrian exile and had not returned as a people, some individual descendants likely had returned. Anna serves as their representative. Simeon, on the other hand, lives in Jerusalem and is likely a native Judean. Thus, Luke depicts representatives of both the Northern and Southern Kingdoms as longing for, and declaring, the redemption of Israel.

Although some scholars suggest that Luke diminishes Anna's role since Simeon alone has a lengthy monologue, Luke actually heightens Anna's status in other ways. Whereas Simeon is generally described as righteous and full of the Holy Spirit, Anna is specifically called a prophet. Whereas Simeon is led into the temple by the Holy Spirit, Anna is already there, worshipping night and day with prayers and fasting. Whereas Simeon speaks only to Mary and Joseph, Anna prophesies publicly to all who are waiting for the redemption of Israel.

Thus Anna joins the ranks of other female prophets (Miriam, Deborah, Huldah, Isaiah's wife, and, as Luke will later describe in Acts, the four daughters of Phillip) who proclaim God's word to a people longing for hope.

1. Although many women in Scripture are identified by their roles as wives and mothers, this was not the case for Anna. What was her primary role?

2. What appears to be the main focus of Anna's prayers and prophecy? How might this instruct us on how we should pray?

3. There were many people in the temple that day. Why were Simeon and Anna the only ones who recognized the Messiah?

FOUR

Mary: Dangerous Faith (Part Two)

Matthew 2:9–15 ESV *After listening to the king, they went on their way. And behold, the star that they had seen when it rose went before them until it came to rest over the place where the child was. ¹⁰When they saw the star, they rejoiced exceedingly with great joy. ¹¹And going into the house, they saw the child with Mary his mother, and they fell down and worshiped him. Then, opening their treasures, they offered him gifts, gold and frankincense and myrrh. ¹²And being warned in a dream not to return to Herod, they departed to their own country by another way.*

¹³*Now when they had departed, behold, an angel of the Lord appeared to Joseph in a dream and said, "Rise, take the child and his mother, and flee to Egypt, and remain there until I tell you, for Herod is about to search for the child, to destroy him." ¹⁴And he rose and took the child and his mother by night and departed to Egypt ¹⁵and remained there until the death of Herod. This was to fulfill what the Lord had spoken by the prophet, "Out of Egypt I called my son."*

Read all of Matthew 2:1–23.

Key Observation. God's plans often meet with resistance in the world.

Understanding the Word. Unlike Luke, Matthew does not focus on the joy of Jesus' birth. Instead, he only briefly mentions the birth (1:25) and fast-forwards almost two years to focus on the tense political implications resulting from the Messiah's entry into the world. Joseph and Mary have remained in Bethlehem. Were they avoiding the stigma in Nazareth of Mary's pre-wedding pregnancy? Magi from the east have come to nearby Jerusalem and begin asking troubling questions. Matthew does not tell us how many magi appeared, nor does he describe them as royalty ("We Three Kings" is a later invention). Rather, these men are likely astrologers from Persia or Babylon. They had witnessed some kind of phenomenon among the stars nearly two years earlier and interpreted it as a sign pointing to a child born King of the Jews. (Scientists have argued about what the magi might have seen in the night sky; it may be best simply to describe it as a miraculous message from God.) These foreigners may not have heard the reputation of Herod the Great: he is a paranoid ruler who is willing to kill his own sons to retain his power. When they naively ask Herod about a *different* King of the Jews, they do not recognize the firestorm they have created.

After receiving direction from Herod to head to Bethlehem, the magi arrive at Mary and Joseph's doorstep. The couple that had only been able to give the offering of the poor in the temple two years earlier now receive extravagant gifts. By naming the gifts, Matthew may be foreshadowing Jesus' death: frankincense and myrrh were expensive ingredients often used in burial rites. Mary and Joseph will soon discover that their newfound wealth will help them afford their last-minute trip to Egypt. Shortly after the magi leave for their homeland (avoiding Herod in response to a divinely sent dream), an angel of the Lord warns Joseph in the middle of the night to take his family and flee to

Egypt because Herod is looking for Jesus to kill him. Joseph does not wait until morning, but immediately takes his wife and toddler and leaves in the dark for Egypt. They remain as refugees there until after Herod's death and, even then, Joseph will not go back to Judea. He fears Herod's son, who is now ruling there. As a result, the Savior of the world will grow up in Nazareth, in the northern region of Galilee.

Matthew does not give Mary a voice in this story; rather, he focuses on the fulfillment of prophecy and Joseph's obedience to God. Joseph protects his wife and adopted son every step of the way. One may wonder whether the couple, on their return to their homeland, hear the stories of babies slaughtered in Bethlehem several months earlier. The joy of the Messiah's birth has become tainted with the horror of a world not ready for change.

1. In what ways did Mary's story turn from triumph to tragedy?

2. What does the world's resistance to the gospel tell us about the nature of God's plans?

3. How did Mary and Joseph work together to accomplish God's plans? How does this provide a model for other marriages?

FIVE

Mary: Parenting Woes (Part Three)

Luke 2:43–50 *When the festival was ended and they started to return, the boy Jesus stayed behind in Jerusalem, but his parents did not know it. ⁴⁴Assuming that he was in the group of travelers, they went a day's journey. Then they started to look for him among their relatives and friends. ⁴⁵When they did not find him, they returned to Jerusalem to search for him. ⁴⁶After three days they found him in the temple, sitting among the teachers, listening to them and asking them questions. ⁴⁷And all who heard him were amazed at his understanding and his answers. ⁴⁸When his parents saw him they were astonished; and his mother said to him, "Child, why have you treated us like this? Look, your father and I have been searching for you in great anxiety." ⁴⁹He said to them, "Why were you searching for me? Did you not know that I must be in my Father's house?" ⁵⁰But they did not understand what he said to them.*

John 2:1–5 *On the third day there was a wedding in Cana of Galilee, and the mother of Jesus was there. ²Jesus and his disciples had also been invited to the wedding. ³When the wine gave out, the mother of Jesus said to him, "They have no wine." ⁴And Jesus said to her, "Woman, what concern is that to you and to me? My hour has not yet come." ⁵His mother said to the servants, "Do whatever he tells you."*

Read also Mark 3:19b–21, 31–35; John 2:6–11, 19:25b–27; and Acts 1:14.

Key Observation. God's calling upon your life may differ from the expectations of others, even within your own family.

Understanding the Word. Scripture regularly presents Jesus as misunderstood, even by his own family. The first time we see this dynamic, the family has been traveling in a caravan back to Nazareth after celebrating the Passover festival in Jerusalem. Mary and Joseph suddenly discover that twelve-year-old Jesus is not with anyone else in the caravan. After frantic searching, they eventually find Jesus in the temple astonishing the teachers with his precocious wisdom. Anger and relief fill Mary's cry: "Child, why have you treated us like this?" But his calm response—"Did you not know that I must be in my Father's house?"—must feel like a slap in the face to Joseph. Joseph knows the temple isn't *his* house (vv. 48–50). Jesus already recognizes that he is not destined to fill his adoptive father's shoes.

By the time Jesus begins his public ministry, Joseph has likely died. Mary struggles to make sense of her son's vocation. She likely has seen Jesus work miracles privately, because she eagerly intervenes when the wine begins to run out at a wedding in Cana. (Mary wants to protect the bridegroom from the dishonor of lacking hospitality for his guests.) She believes Jesus has the ability to help, despite the fact that Jesus is not a vintner! Jesus' response ("My hour has not yet come" in John 2:4) indicates he knows she is asking for a miracle. He is reluctant to reveal himself as Messiah so soon. Nonetheless, his command results in the sudden creation of 120 gallons of wine! Mary may not recognize that this miracle demonstrates the overwhelming abundance of God's provision and alludes to Jesus' key role at the end-times messianic banquet (see Isaiah 25:6).

Mary's pride in her son's powers, however, will soon turn to confusion. As Jesus' teaching and miracles challenge the authority of Jewish leaders, his family will try to stop him. They think he is losing his mind (see Mark 3:21). But Jesus tells the crowds that *they* are his true family when they do the will of God (see Mark 3:33–35). In an era when one's family provides the basis for a person's identity, Jesus' statement would be offensive to Mary and her other sons. Once again, Jesus makes it clear that his destiny follows a different path.

Mary's pain will only increase when she watches her eldest son, the one about whom so many grand promises have been made, die a horrific death on a cross. What has happened to the promises of God? How could *this* be the fate of God's Messiah? Yet, as Jesus is dying, he asks his disciple John to care for Mary (see John 19:25–27). Jesus wants to make sure that his mother will be nurtured, not by his unbelieving brothers, but by his true family—his disciples.

The horrors that Mary witnesses during her lifetime will not become the defining narrative, however. She will soon be counted among the disciples who pray together after the resurrected Jesus ascends into heaven (see Acts 1:14). The promises she had heard so long ago have not been empty after all.

1. In what ways did Mary experience complicated family dynamics?

2. How were God's plans for Jesus different from Mary's plans for her son?

3. Parents and children don't always agree on the direction a child's life should take. How does Jesus' interaction with his mother instruct us about navigating these tensions?

WEEK ONE

GATHERING DISCUSSION OUTLINE

A. **Open session in prayer.** Ask that God would astonish us anew with fresh insight from God's Word and transform us into the disciples that Jesus desires us to become.

B. **View video for this week's readings.**

C. **What were key insights or takeaways that you gained from your reading during the week and from watching the video commentary?** In particular, how did these help you to grow in your faith and understanding of Scripture this week? What parts of the Bible lessons or study raised questions for you?

D. **Discuss selected questions from the daily readings.** Invite class members to share key insights or to raise questions that they found to be the most meaningful.

  1. **KEY OBSERVATION:** Sometimes faith takes a long time to prove true.

     DISCUSSION QUESTION: What are ways to be encouraged and keep the faith when it seems that God is taking a long time to act?

  2. **KEY OBSERVATION:** God's calling can be unexpected and even filled with difficulty.

     DISCUSSION QUESTION: Why do Christians sometimes think God's calling should be easy? How does this passage, as well as other stories in Scripture, correct that viewpoint?

3. **KEY OBSERVATION:** A posture of prayer often leads to revelation.

   DISCUSSION QUESTION: There were many people in the temple that day. Why were Simeon and Anna the only ones who recognized the Messiah?

4. **KEY OBSERVATION:** God's plans often meet with resistance in the world.

   DISCUSSION QUESTION: What does the world's resistance to the gospel tell us about the nature of God's plans? *God's word is based on facts. The world is the devel laws*

5. **KEY OBSERVATION:** God's calling upon your life may differ from the expectations of others, even within your own family.

   DISCUSSION QUESTION: Parents and children don't always agree on the direction a child's life should take. How does Jesus' interaction with his mother instruct us about navigating these tensions?

E. **As the study concludes, consider specific ways that this week's Bible lessons invite you to grow and call you to change.** How do they call us to think differently? How do they challenge us to change in order to align ourselves with God's work in the world? What specific actions should we take to apply the insights of the lessons into our daily lives? What kind of person do our Bible lessons call us to become?

F. **Close session with prayer.** Emphasize God's ongoing work of transformation in our lives in preparation for loving mission and service in the world. Pray for absent class members as well as for persons whom we need to invite to join our study.

WEEK TWO

Jesus' Treatment of Women

ONE

The Daughter of Jairus and the Bleeding Woman

Luke 8:41–48, 51–55a NIV *Then a man named Jairus, a synagogue leader, came and fell at Jesus' feet, pleading with him to come to his house* [42]*because his only daughter, a girl of about twelve, was dying.*

As Jesus was on his way, the crowds almost crushed him. [43]*And a woman was there who had been subject to bleeding for twelve years, but no one could heal her.* [44]*She came up behind him and touched the edge of his cloak, and immediately her bleeding stopped.*

[45]*"Who touched me?" Jesus asked.*

When they all denied it, Peter said, "Master, the people are crowding and pressing against you."

[46]*But Jesus said, "Someone touched me; I know that power has gone out from me."*

[47]*Then the woman, seeing that she could not go unnoticed, came trembling and fell at his feet. In the presence of all the people, she told why she had touched him and how she had been instantly healed.* [48]*Then he said to her, "Daughter, your faith has healed you. Go in peace."* . . .

[51]*When he arrived at the house of Jairus, he did not let anyone go in with him except Peter, John and James, and the child's father and mother.* [52]*Meanwhile, all the people were wailing and mourning for her. "Stop wailing," Jesus said. "She is not dead but asleep."*

⁵³They laughed at him, knowing that she was dead. ⁵⁴But he took her by the hand and said, "My child, get up!" ⁵⁵Her spirit returned, and at once she stood up. . . .

Read also Matthew 9:18–26 and Mark 5:21–43.

Key Observation. Jesus shares his grace with all people, regardless of their social status.

Understanding the Word. In the first century, a person's status was determined by a number of factors. Race, gender, wealth, and reputation all played a role. When Jesus came on the scene, however, he ignored the unspoken rules of society. Whether a person was a Jew or a Gentile, a man or a woman, rich or poor, honorable or outcast, Jesus ministered to them all.

The story of the synagogue ruler and the bleeding woman underscores Jesus' willingness to heal all people. Although Luke could tell separate stories, he intentionally wraps the tale of the bleeding woman within the report of the raising of Jairus's daughter. Jairus is the kind of man one would want to help: he has status in the community; he is a leader in the synagogue, the center of Jewish worship. Yet his reputation alone cannot save his twelve-year-old daughter from illness. Casting all honor aside, Jairus begs Jesus for help. Jesus is more than willing and starts in that direction.

Then Jesus gets interrupted. Luke introduces us to a woman sneaking through the crowd trying to get to Jesus. For as long as Jairus's daughter has been alive, this woman has felt like she was dying. Her period has flowed non-stop for twelve years. The pain and exhaustion has taken its toll; she has spent all her money on doctors and the best medicine hasn't worked. Now she is poor and an outcast. In her culture, a flow of blood makes a person ritually unclean. Anyone who comes in contact with her would also become unclean and would need to perform religious rituals to cleanse the impurity. Who would want to draw near to a woman like that? Luckily the crowd has not noticed her or they would be upset that she is in their midst. The woman reaches out to touch the edge of Jesus' cloak. Immediately, she is healed.

Before she can sneak away, however, Jesus exclaims, "Someone touched me!" (v. 46). Peter, confused, points out that everyone is bumping into Jesus!

But not everyone has received his power. It is startling to think that people can brush up against Jesus and yet gain nothing from him. Only the ones who reach out will receive. Jesus addresses the issue because he wants the crowd to know who has received his gift. This lonely outcast has had great faith and he applauds her after she proclaims her story. Jesus has just reinstated her into the community.

Meanwhile, Jairus is panic-stricken at the delay, and his worst fears are confirmed when servants arrive to inform him of his daughter's death. But Jesus challenges Jairus to have the same kind of faith as the outcast woman. Although the crowds at the house mock Jesus when he says the girl is only sleeping, their derision soon turns to astonishment. Jesus has power over even death.

Luke intertwines these stories because he wants his readers to see that the power of Jesus is available to all who believe, whether rich or poor, male or female, reputable or outcast.

1. How are Jairus and the bleeding woman different? How are they alike?

2. What is the difference between those who casually bump into Jesus and those who receive miraculous gifts?

3. In what ways can you share Christ's love with those who may move in different social circles than you?

TWO

The Widow of Nain

Luke 7:11–17 ESV *Soon afterward he went to a town called Nain, and his disciples and a great crowd went with him. *[12]*As he drew near to the gate of the town, behold, a man who had died was being carried out, the only son of his mother, and she was a widow, and a considerable crowd from the town was with her. *[13]*And when the Lord saw her, he had compassion on her and said to her, "Do not weep." *[14]*Then he came up and touched the bier, and the bearers stood still. And he said, "Young man, I say to you, arise." *[15]*And the dead man sat up and began to speak, and Jesus gave him to his mother. *[16]*Fear seized them all, and they glorified God, saying, "A great prophet has arisen among us!" and "God has visited* *his people!" ¹⁷And this report about him spread through the whole of Judea and all the surrounding country.*

Key Observation. Compassion is an action, not just a feeling.

Understanding the Word. Jesus never performs miracles to provide a show for the people or as a means of seeking attention. Rather, his miracles demonstrate both his compassion for the needy and his God-given power to bring the kingdom to a hurting world.

In this case, a widow's only son has just died. Her grief must be overwhelming. She has lost a beloved son, but this loss involves more than a family member. As a widow, her only male protector and provider was her son. Now that this *only* son has died, her economic situation will be desperate. Will she have to beg for food? Will others try to take advantage of her? What will she do now?

Although the Old Testament regularly tells the people of God to care for widows (e.g., Deuteronomy 14:28–29; 24:19–21), the prophets rebuked the people because they failed to do so (e.g., Malachi 3:5; Isaiah 10:1–2). This widow cannot be certain that others will care for her.

Then Jesus arrives. Often Jesus performs miracles because people have great faith. In this case, however, the widow has not asked Jesus for help nor has she shown any signs of faith. She may not have even seen Jesus approach through the crowds! Instead, Jesus sees her desperate circumstances and is moved with compassion. The word "compassion" often refers in the Old Testament to God's faithfulness and lovingkindness. This kind of compassion is an *action*, not just a feeling. And so Jesus acts. He tells the woman not to weep, and before anyone can comment on that unrealistic request, Jesus gives her reason to rejoice. He touches the plank on which the man's body is being carried and simply commands the corpse to arise. When the man sits up and speaks, Jesus gives the man back to his mother.

Understandably, everyone responds with a mixture of fear and joy. Coming face-to-face with such power terrifies the people, but they recognize that God is present in this miracle. They have reason to see it this way: they remember the prophet Elijah, who also raised a widow's son from the dead (see 1 Kings 17:17–24). Luke intentionally connects the two stories. Just as Elijah raised the boy "and gave him to his mother" (1 Kings 17:23), so, too, Jesus raises the son and "gave him to his mother" (Luke 7:15). It is clear, however, that Jesus is greater than Elijah. The prophet had to prostrate himself over the body and repeatedly pray for God to intervene. Here, Jesus simply commands the man to arise—and he does! The people are astonished and glorify God.

Immediately following this story, disciples of John the Baptist come and ask Jesus if he is the Messiah. Jesus responds that the blind now see, the lame walk, lepers receive cleansing, the deaf hear, the dead are raised, and the poor hear the good news (Luke 7:22). These miracles of Jesus fulfill Isaiah's prophecies (see Isaiah 26:19; 29:18; 61:1–2), affirming that Jesus' ministry is from God. The widow of Nain not only received her son back to life, but this miracle also played a larger role in proclaiming Jesus as the Christ.

1. Why does Jesus feel compassion for the widow?

2. Why is action a necessary part of compassion?

3. In what ways might Jesus be feeling compassion for your life circumstances?

THREE

The Woman with a Bent Back

Luke 13:10–17 NIV *On a Sabbath Jesus was teaching in one of the synagogues, ¹¹and a woman was there who had been crippled by a spirit for eighteen years. She was bent over and could not straighten up at all. ¹²When Jesus saw her, he called her forward and said to her, "Woman, you are set free from your infirmity." ¹³Then he put his hands on her, and immediately she straightened up and praised God.*

¹⁴Indignant because Jesus had healed on the Sabbath, the synagogue leader said to the people, "There are six days for work. So come and be healed on those days, not on the Sabbath."

¹⁵The Lord answered him, "You hypocrites! Doesn't each of you on the Sabbath untie your ox or donkey from the stall and lead it out to give it water? ¹⁶Then should not this woman, a daughter of Abraham, whom Satan has kept bound for eighteen long years, be set free on the Sabbath day from what bound her?"

¹⁷When he said this, all his opponents were humiliated, but the people were delighted with all the wonderful things he was doing.

Key Observation. The liberation Jesus brings sometimes confronts our religious traditions.

Understanding the Word. Synagogues were places where Jewish community members met together to praise God, hear the Scriptures being read, receive teaching, and pray. On this Sabbath day, a synagogue leader has asked Jesus to teach. One of the community members listening to him is a woman who is severely disabled; her spine is so warped that she cannot stand up straight. How difficult it is for her to look someone in the face! Luke's description makes it clear that this is not simply a physical problem, but there is a spiritual component as well. This woman is broken in many ways. But despite the problems she has been facing for eighteen long years, she still comes to the synagogue to hear the Word of God. Can she even see Jesus through the crowds, given her deformed stature?

It doesn't matter, because Jesus sees her. He calls her forward in front of the whole community. Her—a woman with only brokenness to offer! Jesus doesn't quiz her or ask her about her faith. Before she can say a word, he declares that she is set free from her illness. When he lays his hands on her, the woman's back immediately straightens. Her constant pain is gone and she can look her friends and family in the eyes once again. She has no doubt about what just happened; she immediately begins glorifying God for this miracle.

But then she hears the synagogue ruler. He is too cowardly to address Jesus directly, so instead he tells the community that they should not come for healing on the Sabbath when work is forbidden. They should come on the other six days of the week. He is publicly blaming her for causing the Sabbath rules to be broken. But she didn't even ask for this! It was a gift of God. Surely God wouldn't violate his own holy day?

Jesus is not done with her yet. The synagogue ruler is indignant, but nothing can match the look on Jesus' face, which she can finally see. Now Jesus publicly shames the synagogue ruler and all of the other elders who agreed with him. Jesus calls them hypocrites! He is angry that they treat their animals better than they have treated this woman. These men allow exceptions to the

Law to take care of their animals, but they won't allow an exception for her. Jesus then points at her and calls her a "daughter of Abraham" (v. 16). She is part of the covenant people of God. She is family! If an animal can be unbound on the Sabbath, then surely a family member can be unbound from Satan's torments. Why would God wait even a day to break Satan's hold? Why should Satan get a reprieve on the holy Sabbath? This is the Lord's day, and everyone must know who is Lord.

The woman's honor and dignity are restored. In a patriarchal society, Jesus has just affirmed the value of women and he challenges the men in the community to reorder their priorities based on God's values, not their own cultural bias.

1. How might the woman have felt during the various twists and turns of this conversation?

2. Why is it important to keep religious rules? When is it important to ignore religious rules?

3. Which traditions or rules in your church sometimes prevent you from fully valuing or ministering to a person in need?

FOUR

The Canaanite Woman

Matthew 15:21–28 *Jesus left that place and went away to the district of Tyre and Sidon.* *²²Just then a Canaanite woman from that region came out and started shouting, "Have mercy on me, Lord, Son of David; my daughter is tormented by a demon." ²³But he did not answer her at all. And his disciples came and urged him, saying, "Send her away, for she keeps shouting after us." ²⁴He answered, "I was sent only to the lost sheep of the house of Israel." ²⁵But she came and knelt before him, saying, "Lord, help me." ²⁶He answered, "It is not fair to take the children's food and throw it to the dogs." ²⁷She said, "Yes, Lord, yet even the dogs eat the crumbs that fall from their masters' table." ²⁸Then Jesus answered her, "Woman, great is your faith! Let it be done for you as you wish." And her daughter was healed instantly.*

Read also Mark 7:24–30.

Key Observation. Persistent faith is more important than social identity markers like ethnicity and gender.

Understanding the Word. Matthew frames his story as an ethnic issue in multiple ways. He begins by noting that Jesus and his disciples have gone to a region outside of Israel. The woman who approaches them is not Jewish, but Canaanite. Ethnically and theologically, this woman is different. This story surprises the reader because Jesus first ignores the woman and then calls Gentiles "dogs." This is not the kind, compassionate Jesus we have come to expect! Earlier in the Gospel, however, Matthew hinted that foreigners will be accepted when he noted that more than one of Jesus' foremothers were Gentiles (see Matthew 1:1–16).

As the story begins, the unnamed woman approaches Jesus and starts shouting after him. This is no meek, mild woman. Her bold approach to an unfamiliar man demonstrates her desperation; she is willing to defy social norms in order to help her troubled daughter. Yet her boldness is not without respect. Every time she addresses Jesus, she calls him "lord." This is a term of respect (like "sir"). Even though she is not Jewish, she seems to understand Jewish ideas of a coming messiah. She calls Jesus "Son of David" (v. 22), a term the Jews used for the expected messiah who would rule over David's kingdom. Clearly, she has also heard the rumors that Jesus is this promised one. Her daughter is demon-possessed; surely a holy man can help!

Jesus' initial response is quite unsettling. He ignores her plea. This is unusual behavior for Jesus, who does not ignore the cries of the needy. Thus, something else is going on here. Jesus may be hoping she will engage in further dialogue so that everyone will be forced to think about the relationship between these two people groups. The disciples, however, simply see the woman as a nuisance and they ask Jesus to send her away.

When Jesus tells the woman that his mission is focused on Jews and not Gentiles, she is not deterred. She kneels in front of Jesus, begging for help. Jesus repeats his focus on helping Jews; they are the people whom God has chosen to receive special favor and blessings. Jesus uses the metaphor of giving food to children (Jews) and not to dogs (Gentiles).

The woman does not appear to be offended. Even though she has been rebuffed twice, she is no quitter. Instead, the woman uses Jesus' own metaphor to encourage him to help her: even the dogs under the table get a few crumbs from their master ("lord"). In one fell swoop she includes herself as a member of God's household! Theologically, this is not a new idea. In Genesis 12:3, God promised that all the peoples of the earth would be blessed through Abraham. The woman lays claim to this promise.

Jesus publicly applauds the woman's great faith and grants her request. At that hour, her daughter is healed. The unnamed foreign woman engaged in a theological debate with the Jewish Messiah—and won!

1. When have you felt like an outsider? Why did others receive special treatment and you did not?

2. How does this story address the tensions between different people groups? What is most important to Jesus?

3. Which social norms do you find most difficult to look past? How might God be calling you to repent?

FIVE

Martha and Mary

Luke 10:38b–42 ESV *And a woman named Martha welcomed him into her house. ³⁹And she had a sister called Mary, who sat at the Lord's feet and listened to his teaching. ⁴⁰But Martha was distracted with much serving. And she went up to him and said, "Lord, do you not care that my sister has left me to serve alone? Tell her then to help me." ⁴¹But the Lord answered her, "Martha, Martha, you are anxious and troubled about many things, ⁴²but one thing is necessary. Mary has chosen the good portion, which will not be taken away from her."*

John 11:20–27 ESV *So when Martha heard that Jesus was coming, she went and met him, but Mary remained seated in the house. ²¹Martha said to Jesus, "Lord, if you had been here, my brother would not have died. ²²But even now I know that whatever you ask from God, God will give you." ²³Jesus said to her, "Your brother will rise again." ²⁴Martha said to him, "I know that he will rise again in the resurrection on the last day." ²⁵Jesus said to her, "I am the resurrection and the life. Whoever believes in me, though he die, yet shall he live, ²⁶and everyone who lives and believes in me shall never die. Do you believe this?" ²⁷She* *said to him, "Yes, Lord; I believe that you are the Christ, the Son of God, who is coming into the world."*

John 12:2b–3a ESV *Martha served, and Lazarus was one of those reclining with him at the table. ³Mary therefore took a pound of expensive ointment made from pure nard, and anointed the feet of Jesus and wiped his feet with her hair.*

Read all of John 11:1–44 and John 12:1–8.

Key Observation. Different personalities serve the kingdom in different ways.

Understanding the Word. Although Martha and Mary are sisters, they express their faith in very different ways. Martha is the assertive one who will not take no for an answer. Mary is the contemplative one whose creativity leads her to take social risks. Jesus' interactions with these disciples demonstrate the high esteem he has for both women.

Luke describes the story of Martha hosting Jesus at her home. Instead of helping her sister, Mary takes the position of a disciple sitting at the feet of Jesus to learn. This is a huge social breach—normally women and men were separated and rabbis did not welcome women as students! Furthermore, Martha is so concerned with providing hospitality that she interrupts the teaching to scold both Jesus ("do you not care . . . ?") and Mary. Despite calling Jesus "Lord," Martha is clearly telling him what to do (v. 40). Jesus, however, gently chides her. It's not that Martha's desire to show hospitality is wrong; rather, she has let her service become more important than the one whom she is serving. In the larger scope of Luke's narrative, the emphasis on Mary's contemplative faith balances the emphasis on active faith in the preceding story (the good Samaritan). Both doing and listening are a necessary part of kingdom life.

Martha's assertive personality also appears in John 11. The sisters had sent word to Jesus that their brother, Lazarus, was ill. Jesus had delayed in coming; by the time he arrives, Lazarus is dead and buried. Although Mary remains in the house grieving, Martha does not waste a moment and she heads out to meet Jesus. Her first words to Jesus reflect the complexity of emotions that grief brings: "Lord, if you had been here, my brother would not have died. But even now, I know that whatever you ask from God, God will give you" (v. 22). She is angry that the Healer didn't make her brother's illness a priority, but yet she still believes in Jesus. As they discuss end-times resurrection, Jesus reassures Martha that the power of eternal life stands before her now. She responds by boldly affirming that Jesus is the Son of God. The bustling woman of service has a deep theological understanding.

Martha then goes and calls for her sister. Whereas Martha stood to confront Jesus, Mary falls at his feet. She, too, cries out, "Lord, if you had been here, my brother would not have died" (v. 32). Mary does not engage in theological conversation; she simply weeps with the crowd of mourners. Jesus joins in their weeping. Moved by the suffering, he approaches the tomb. With a loud cry, Jesus overcomes death itself as Lazarus stumbles out to new life.

The last story of the sisters again shows Martha serving (John 12:2). Mary once again challenges societal expectations. She opens a jar of perfume worth almost a year's wages and anoints Jesus' feet, wiping them with her hair. It was certainly a social misstep for a woman to let down her hair in public, let alone to waste such an extravagant gift! But Jesus praises Mary's creative act of devotion.

1. In what ways do each of these women serve the kingdom?

2. How do the sisters grieve differently? How does Jesus respond?

3. What do you appreciate about the kingdom service of people whose personalities and gifts differ from your own?

WEEK TWO

GATHERING DISCUSSION OUTLINE

A. **Open session in prayer.** Ask that God would astonish us anew with fresh insight from God's Word and transform us into the disciples that Jesus desires us to become.

B. **View video for this week's readings.**

C. **What were key insights or takeaways that you gained from your reading during the week and from watching the video commentary?** In particular, how did these help you to grow in your faith and understanding of Scripture this week? What parts of the Bible lessons or study raised questions for you?

D. **Discuss selected questions from the daily readings.** Invite class members to share key insights or to raise questions that they found to be the most meaningful.

   1. **KEY OBSERVATION:** Jesus shares his grace with all people, regardless of their social status.

   DISCUSSION QUESTION: In what ways can you share Christ's love with those who may move in different social circles than you?

   2. **KEY OBSERVATION:** Compassion is an action, not just a feeling.

   DISCUSSION QUESTION: Why is action a necessary part of compassion?

3. **KEY OBSERVATION:** The liberation Jesus brings sometimes confronts our religious traditions.

   DISCUSSION QUESTION: Which traditions or rules in your church sometimes prevent you from fully valuing or ministering to a person in need?

4. **KEY OBSERVATION:** Persistent faith is more important than social identity markers like ethnicity and gender.

   DISCUSSION QUESTION: Which social norms do you find most difficult to look past? How might God be calling you to repent?

5. **KEY OBSERVATION:** Different personalities serve the kingdom in different ways.

   DISCUSSION QUESTION: What do you appreciate about the kingdom service of people whose personalities and gifts differ from your own?

E. **As the study concludes, consider specific ways that this week's Bible lessons invite you to grow and call you to change.** How do they call us to think differently? How do they challenge us to change in order to align ourselves with God's work in the world? What specific actions should we take to apply the insights of the lessons into our daily lives? What kind of person do our Bible lessons call us to become?

F. **Close session with prayer.** Emphasize God's ongoing work of transformation in our lives in preparation for loving mission and service in the world. Pray for absent class members as well as for persons whom we need to invite to join our study.

Women in Jesus' Teaching

ONE

Teaching on Divorce

Matthew 19:3–9 *Some Pharisees came to him, and to test him they asked, "Is it lawful for a man to divorce his wife for any cause?"* *⁴He answered, "Have you not read that the one who made them at the beginning 'made them male and female,'* *⁵and said, 'For this reason a man shall leave his father and mother and be joined to his wife, and the two shall become one flesh'? ⁶So they are no longer two, but one flesh. Therefore what God has joined together, let no one separate." ⁷They said to him, "Why then did Moses command us to give a certificate of dismissal and to divorce her?" ⁸He said to them, "It was because you were so hard-hearted that Moses allowed you to divorce your wives, but from the beginning it was not so. ⁹And I say to you, whoever divorces his wife, except for unchastity, and marries another commits adultery."*

Read also Matthew 5:31–32; Mark 10:2–12; and Luke 16:18.

Key Observation. Rather than asking how to get out of a marriage, Jesus instructs believers to focus on how to stay in a marriage.

Understanding the Word. Jesus refers to women in a number of ways in his teachings. Women provide positive role models, women's actions serve as a metaphor for God's love, and Jesus protects women from inequitable laws. His teaching on divorce provides a prime example of the latter. In the first century, Jewish men could divorce their wives, but women could not normally divorce their husbands. (In the Greco-Roman world, both husbands and wives could initiate a divorce.) Rabbis debated the legal grounds for divorce. Some argued that a husband could divorce his wife for any reason—even if she burned his food! The wife's only legal protection was that she would receive any money her husband had pledged at the time of marriage. But in a world where a woman's provision came through men, easy divorce often left women with nothing but a desperate future.

Jesus' restrictive view of divorce thus provided protection for women. His teaching, however, can be confusing. In Mark and Luke, Jesus prohibits divorce without exception. But in Matthew, Jesus allows divorce in the case of unfaithfulness. So does Jesus allow divorce or not?

It is important to recognize the context of the Gospel stories. Except for Matthew 5:31–32, Jesus is responding to Pharisees who are trying to test or ridicule him. They are asking about loopholes in marriage laws, and Jesus responds by changing the emphasis of the question. Rather than explaining how to get out of a marriage, Jesus proclaims that God intends for a man and a woman to remain committed to one another. He refers to the Genesis creation narrative to support his viewpoint; the sexual union in marriage creates a unique bond that should not be broken. Thus, the focus should be on how to stay together, not how to separate. Nonetheless, Jesus does suggest that unfaithfulness can terminate a marriage. Likely he does not offer other exceptions because to do so would support the Pharisees' way of thinking. (Elsewhere in Scripture other exceptions appear. For example, Paul allows divorce in the case of an unbelieving spouse in 1 Corinthians 7:15. One could make the argument from other passages that domestic violence provides another exception.)

Even the more restrictive passages actually provide significant protections for women. In Mark 10:11, Jesus says that a man who divorces his wife and marries another commits adultery against her. This is a stunning statement, because the Old Testament defined adultery as a man having sex with another man's wife. Under that definition, a man does not commit adultery against *his own* wife. (For example, in the ancient world men often had sex with prostitutes but did not consider it adultery against their wives.) Jesus clearly states that a man *does* commit adultery against his wife! Jesus also goes further than the rabbis when he tells men that if they look lustfully at another woman, they have already committed adultery in their hearts (see Matthew 5:28).

Thus, Jesus counterculturally argues for a marriage commitment that protects both partners and prevents women from being casually cast aside.

1. How would men and women have responded differently to Jesus' teaching about divorce?

2. In modern society, do you think men or women fare worse in divorce? Why?

3. How do Jesus' teachings about divorce still provide a countercultural viewpoint?

TWO

The Woman with Two Coins

Mark 12:41–44 NIV *Jesus sat down opposite the place where the offerings were put and watched the crowd putting their money into the temple treasury. Many rich people threw in large amounts. ⁴²But a poor widow came and put in two very small copper coins, worth only a few cents.*

⁴³Calling his disciples to him, Jesus said, "Truly I tell you, this poor widow has put more into the treasury than all the others. ⁴⁴They all gave out of their wealth; but she, out of her poverty, put in everything—all she had to live on."

Read also Luke 21:1–4.

Key Observation. Love God with everything you have and hold nothing back.

Understanding the Word. Jesus is teaching in the temple courts during the last week of his life. The Pharisees and the Sadducees have tried to trap Jesus in his words, but Jesus continues to evade their snares. In various ways in Mark 12, Jesus teaches that people must love God with their whole being. He cites the Shema, the basic creed of the Jews found in Deuteronomy 6:4–5. Jesus declares that it calls one to "love the Lord your God with all your heart and with all your soul and with all your mind and with all your strength" (Matt. 12:30). When asked about paying taxes to the Roman government, Jesus asks about the image found on Roman coins. He then tells the people to pay to

Caesar what is Caesar's and pay to God what is God's (see Matthew 12:17). In so doing, he reminds them that all people are stamped with the image of God. Thus, we belong to God and owe God everything.

Shortly after this, Jesus sits down in the outer court of the temple and watches people throw their offerings into the collection box, which has a rams-horn–shaped funnel at the top of the box. Anyone listening to the sound that the coins made as they fell through the funnel would have an idea of how much money had been offered. The repeated clunking noises of the heavy coins of the wealthy would certainly contrast with the light and tinny noise of the two coins of the widow. Mark records that the widow's coins are the very smallest denomination, worth less than two percent of a day's wages. (That's less than one dollar by today's standards.) Yet this is all the poor widow has.

When Jesus witnesses this great sacrifice, he realizes that she is the perfect example of his teaching a few minutes earlier. She loves God with everything she has, holding nothing back. For the wealthy, it would be easy to give the required portion to God and think that is enough; they could do whatever they wanted with the rest. But Jesus advocates a life of total devotion to God. This does not mean that everyone should be poor. Rather, everyone should have an attitude of poverty; we must recognize that nothing we have is our own. It belongs to God and should be used in accordance with God's will.

It probably is not lost on the disciples that Jesus had warned them a few minutes earlier about the teachers of the religious law, who "devour widows' houses" (12:40). The religious leaders were supposed to protect and provide for the poor, but they took advantage of their ability to manage the estate of widows. They helped themselves rather than helped the poor. Jesus critiques their selfish attitude by holding up this poor woman as the epitome of virtue.

1. Why does the amount of your offering not matter as much as the spirit with which it is given?

2. Why is it sometimes difficult to have a sacrificial attitude?

3. What parts of your life are you tempted to hold back from God and why?

THREE

Parable of the Persistent Widow

Luke 18:1–8 *Then Jesus told them a parable about their need to pray always and not to lose heart. ²He said, "In a certain city there was a judge who neither feared God nor had respect for people. ³In that city there was a widow who kept coming to him and saying, 'Grant me justice against my opponent.' ⁴For a while he refused; but later he said to himself, 'Though I have no fear of God and no respect for anyone, ⁵yet because this widow keeps bothering me, I will grant her justice, so that she may not wear me out by continually coming.'" ⁶And the Lord said, "Listen to what the unjust judge says. ⁷And will not God grant justice to his chosen ones who cry to him day and night? Will he delay long in helping them? ⁸I tell you, he will quickly grant justice to them. And yet, when the Son of Man comes, will he find faith on earth?"*

Key Observation. We must patiently wait for the lasting justice that Christ will bring when he returns.

Understanding the Word. Jesus tells his disciples this parable just after he discusses the time of his return (17:20–37). He has just warned them that his coming will be sudden; others will be carrying on with their normal lives when Jesus returns. He has reassured his disciples to remain faithful while they wait. This parable, then, provides encouragement as part of his overall teaching about the end times.

As Jesus lays out his story, he chooses two contradictory characters. On the one hand, he describes a judge who does not fear God or respect the people. In other words, this judge does the opposite of what God requires. (In Luke's Gospel, Jesus has already affirmed that love of God and neighbor are necessary for eternal life. Here Jesus describes a judge who does neither.) On the other hand, Jesus describes a widow in need of justice. Although Jesus does not describe her social situation, he may be using the common stereotype of a poor widow. The judge has power and authority, whereas the widow has little power or social standing. The judge has no compassion or desire to follow God's call to provide for widows and she has no leverage. Those listening to Jesus would assume that her situation is hopeless.

The widow, however, surprises everyone with her bold tenacity. She is not afraid to enter the male realm of the courts, which in the Middle East was a place of pushing and shouting rather than quiet respect. She shouts for justice louder than anyone, day after day. Although the judge tries to ignore her, the woman's persistence eventually wears him down. He is motivated purely by self-interest; out of self-preservation he gets rid of this nuisance by giving the woman what she wants.

The parable may seem to provide an odd comparison between a gracious God and an unjust judge. Jesus often told stories, however, that implied "how much more than this will God do for you?" If a heartless judge responds favorably to persistent pleas for justice, then how much more favorably will our loving God respond to similar pleas?

The parable does not promise that all prayers will be answered in the way we desire. Rather, the context applies to those who are waiting for justice in the interim period before Christ returns. The faithful will be rewarded if they do not give up hope. When the church is persecuted and doubts arise, Jesus encourages believers to keep the faith. And the model he uses to demonstrate this strength is a woman whom no one would ever expect to beat the odds.

1. How does the teaching of Jesus in Luke 17 help you to understand this parable better?

2. Do you ever doubt God's justice? Why is it sometimes difficult to be patient with God and persistent in prayer?

3. What injustices is the church currently suffering and how can you pray to God regarding these issues?

FOUR

Parable of the Ten Bridesmaids

Matthew 25:1–13 ESV *"Then the kingdom of heaven will be like ten virgins who took their lamps and went to meet the bridegroom. ²Five of them were foolish, and five were wise. ³For when the foolish took their lamps, they took no oil with them, ⁴but the wise took flasks of oil with their lamps. ⁵As the bridegroom was delayed, they all became drowsy and slept. ⁶But at midnight there was a cry,*

'Here is the bridegroom! Come out to meet him.' ⁷*Then all those virgins rose and trimmed their lamps. ⁸And the foolish said to the wise, 'Give us some of your oil, for our lamps are going out.' ⁹But the wise answered, saying, 'Since there will not be enough for us and for you, go rather to the dealers and buy for yourselves.' ¹⁰And while they were going to buy, the bridegroom came, and those who were ready went in with him to the marriage feast, and the door was shut. ¹¹Afterward the other virgins came also, saying, 'Lord, lord, open to us.' ¹²But he answered, 'Truly, I say to you, I do not know you.' ¹³Watch therefore, for you know neither the day nor the hour."*

Key Observation. Preparing for the return of Christ involves sharing the gospel and helping those in need.

Understanding the Word. Jesus has been teaching about the signs of the end of the age, stating that no one will know the time of his return (see Matthew 24:36). He gives examples of both men and women who are not ready for the mighty acts of God (24:39–41). Jesus describes a servant who becomes drunk and abusive after he discovers his master will arrive late. He is unprepared for his master's early return and suffers the consequences (24:45–51).

In the parable of the ten bridesmaids (or "virgins"), Jesus likens his return to a wedding celebration. First-century Jews would be familiar with Scripture that compares God to a bridegroom (e.g., Isaiah 54:4–6; 62:4–5; Ezekiel 16:7–34; Hosea 2:19). Now Jesus describes the coming kingdom of heaven—that is, his own return—in the same way. But in this parable, Jesus uses female figures to depict his disciples. Jesus calls to mind the typical wedding banquets of the day in which the groom and his friends would come to the bride's home. There they would accompany the bride and her bridesmaids back to the groom's home for a ceremony and great banquet. In Jesus' story, however, the bridegroom is delayed late into the night. The bridesmaids need oil lamps for the processional. Half of the women have planned ahead by bringing extra oil, while half have not. The unprepared bridesmaids ask for oil from their friends, who wisely refuse. If they share their oil, then all the lamps will go out. Instead, the unprepared women must find a shop to buy more oil. By the time they return, the doors to the banquet are closed. In a shocking twist, the bridegroom does not recognize the women and will not let them enter the banquet.

Jesus makes it clear that simply hanging out with a group of Christians is not enough to prepare one for the kingdom. Rather, his disciples must be spiritually prepared. They cannot grow lazy and abusive like the wicked servant, and they cannot be unprepared like the five foolish bridesmaids. Rather, the ones who enter the kingdom are those who are actively involved in kingdom-making now. Jesus' last two parables clarify what this involves. In Matthew 25:14–30, servants are given money before the master goes on a trip; when the master returns, he rewards those who have invested the money and multiplied the funds. The implication is that the gospel must be shared with others according to one's abilities. The final parable (vv. 31–46) describes the Son of Man sitting on his throne, separating people like sheep and goats. Those who enter the kingdom are the ones who cared for "the least of these brothers and sisters of mine" (v. 40) by feeding, clothing, and visiting them.

Thus, the wise bridesmaids in 25:1–13 represent those who ready themselves for the return of Christ by sharing both spiritual truth and physical help with those in need. By using female characters—some who are foolish and some who are wise—Jesus shows that wisdom is not defined by gender, but by faithfulness to his teachings.

1. In what ways can believers be unprepared for the return of Christ?

2. Do you find it easier to share the gospel through words or through actions? Why?

3. In what ways can you and your church do more to prepare for the return of Christ?

FIVE

Parable of the Lost Coin

Luke 15:8–10 NIV *"Or suppose a woman has ten silver coins and loses one. Doesn't she light a lamp, sweep the house and search carefully until she finds it? ⁹And when she finds it, she calls her friends and neighbors together and says, 'Rejoice with me; I have found my lost coin.' ¹⁰In the same way, I tell you, there is rejoicing in the presence of the angels of God over one sinner who repents."*

Key Observation. The abundance of God's love results in seeking the lost and rejoicing greatly when they return to God.

Understanding the Word. This is the second of three parables that Jesus tells in response to Pharisees who criticize him for befriending sinners (15:1–2). The Pharisees were very concerned to honor God by keeping all of God's commandments, and their zest for purity often led them to avoid those who were not as strict. The parables of the lost sheep (15:3–7) and the lost son (15:11–32), along with this story, underscore Jesus' response: God seeks lost sinners and rejoices when they return to God. This implicitly criticizes the Pharisees for turning away from sinners.

Although Luke does not describe the woman in this parable in detail, she is clearly not wealthy. She only lights one lamp in order to search her whole small house. Furthermore, she only has ten drachmas, and each coin is worth a day's wages. That's not much of a retirement plan. When you have very little to live on, losing a tenth of it becomes all the more significant. And so the woman searches diligently until she finds what she lost. She is so overjoyed that she calls together her friends and neighbors to celebrate with her. Jesus likens this to the great celebration in heaven when a sinner repents.

All three parables provide metaphors for God's abundant, unceasing love. Yet it is striking that one of these metaphors provides female imagery for God. This is not unheard of Scripture—elsewhere God is described as a mother bear (Hosea 13:8), a mother eagle (e.g., Psalm 57:1), a woman in labor (e.g., Isaiah 42:14), and a mother caring for her children (e.g., Isaiah 66:13). In addition, Jesus describes himself as a mother hen (Matthew 23:37; Luke 13:34).

The fact that Scripture uses both male and female metaphors to describe God suggests that we should look beyond gender when interpreting these images. God is neither male nor female (although certainly Jesus, in his incarnation, was a male human). Rather, the qualities of the subject should provide the focus of our interpretation: the fierceness of a bear protecting her cubs, the protectiveness of a father watching over his family, the authority of a king, or the gentle love of a mother nursing her child. In the parable of the woman seeking the lost coin, her diligence provides the key comparison. God never gives up seeking those who are lost.

Perhaps one of the most poignant aspects of these parables is the fact that the lost sheep, coin, and son *already* belonged to the shepherd, woman, and father before they were lost. The same is true for sinners, who belonged to God before they were lost. Whereas the Pharisees say to sinners, "You don't belong," God says, "Welcome back!" The abundant, overwhelming love of God could say nothing less.

1. Who do you consider the worst sinners in today's society? Are you more likely to treat them like the Pharisees treated sinners, or like Jesus did? Why?

2. Which metaphor for God speaks to you most powerfully? Why?

3. When have you been most lost in your own life? How did God's immense love draw you closer to God? How can you share this same kind of love with others?

WEEK THREE

GATHERING DISCUSSION OUTLINE

A. **Open session in prayer.** Ask that God would astonish us anew with fresh insight from God's Word and transform us into the disciples that Jesus desires us to become.

B. **View video for this week's readings.**

C. **What were key insights or takeaways that you gained from your reading during the week and from watching the video commentary?** In particular, how did these help you to grow in your faith and understanding of Scripture this week? What parts of the Bible lessons or study raised questions for you?

D. **Discuss selected questions from the daily readings.** Invite class members to share key insights or to raise questions that they found to be the most meaningful.

1. **KEY OBSERVATION:** Rather than asking how to get out of a marriage, Jesus instructs believers to focus on how to stay in a marriage.

   DISCUSSION QUESTION: How do Jesus' teachings about divorce still provide a countercultural viewpoint?

2. **KEY OBSERVATION:** Love God with everything you have and hold nothing back.

   DISCUSSION QUESTION: What parts of your life are you tempted to hold back from God and why?

3. **KEY OBSERVATION:** We must patiently wait for the lasting justice that Christ will bring when he returns.

   DISCUSSION QUESTION: What injustices is the church currently suffering and how can you pray to God regarding these issues?

4. **KEY OBSERVATION:** Preparing for the return of Christ involves sharing the gospel and helping those in need.

   DISCUSSION QUESTION: In what ways can you and your church do more to prepare for the return of Christ?
   Figure out ways to minister to community

5. **KEY OBSERVATION:** The abundance of God's love results in seeking the lost and rejoicing greatly when they return to God.

   DISCUSSION QUESTION: When have you been most lost in your own life? How did God's immense love draw you closer to God? How can you share this same kind of love with others?
   When I had to realize that to forgive is better than feeling put upon.

E. **As the study concludes, consider specific ways that this week's Bible lessons invite you to grow and call you to change.** How do they call us to think differently? How do they challenge us to change in order to align ourselves with God's work in the world? What specific actions should we take to apply the insights of the lessons into our daily lives? What kind of person do our Bible lessons call us to become?
Patient, Forgiving, Giving & Living in God's word actively

F. **Close session with prayer.** Emphasize God's ongoing work of transformation in our lives in preparation for loving mission and service in the world. Pray for absent class members as well as for persons whom we need to invite to join our study.

Female Proclaimers of the Gospel

ONE

The Samaritan Woman at the Well

John 4:19–26, 28–29, 39, 42 NIV *"Sir," the woman said, "I can see that you are a prophet. [20]Our ancestors worshiped on this mountain, but you Jews claim that the place where we must worship is in Jerusalem."*

[21]"Woman," Jesus replied, "believe me, a time is coming when you will worship the Father neither on this mountain nor in Jerusalem. [22]You Samaritans worship what you do not know; we worship what we do know, for salvation is from the Jews. [23]Yet a time is coming and has now come when the true worshipers will worship the Father in the Spirit and in truth, for they are the kind of worshipers the Father seeks. [24]God is spirit, and his worshipers must worship in the Spirit and in truth."

[25]The woman said, "I know that Messiah" (called Christ) "is coming. When he comes, he will explain everything to us."

[26]Then Jesus declared, "I, the one speaking to you—I am he." . . .

[28]Then, leaving her water jar, the woman went back to the town and said to the people, [29]"Come, see a man who told me everything I ever did. Could this be the Messiah?" . . .

[39]Many of the Samaritans from that town believed in him because of the woman's testimony, "He told me everything I ever did." . . .

[42]They said to the woman, "We no longer believe just because of what you said; now we have heard for ourselves, and we know that this man really is the Savior of the world."

Read also John 4:1–18.

Key Observation. Meeting Christ transforms people.

Understanding the Word. In the first century, Jewish rules usually prohibited women from testifying in court. Women were not considered reliable witnesses. Stereotypes in the Greco-Roman world similarly depicted women as weak, irrational, and overly emotional. Surprisingly, then, the New Testament records numerous accounts of women who boldly proclaimed that Jesus is the Christ.

Even more surprising in today's story is the fact that Jesus starts a conversation with a *Samaritan* woman. Hundreds of years earlier when Assyria had conquered Samaria, some Jews had intermarried with foreigners. The other Jews thus no longer considered those Samaritans to be truly Jewish. Theological differences (such as which parts of the Jewish Scriptures were authoritative) also caused conflict. In order to travel from Galilee in the north to Judea in the south, Jews often traveled around Samaria rather than through it. They did not want to risk defilement by the Samaritans. It is no wonder that the Samaritan woman is shocked when Jesus, a Jew, asks to sip from her water jar! But Jesus' question starts a larger conversation about living water (the Holy Spirit) that leads to eternal life (vv. 10, 13).

Other details in the story also point to the woman's status as an outcast. She visits the well in the heat of the day (v. 6), which suggests she is avoiding the other women who would have come to draw water in the cool of the morning. In the ensuing conversation we learn why: the woman has had five husbands and is currently living with a man who is not her husband. Men (and especially rabbis) generally did not speak to women in public, and they certainly would not have spoken to this *kind* of woman!

In addressing her, Jesus thus breaks three different social barriers: gender, ethnicity, and piety. Astonished by his audacity and ashamed that her sinfulness has been revealed, the woman challenges the prophet by picking a theological fight. She raises the question of the proper location for the Jewish temple—a question which has caused deep divisions for hundreds of years. Jesus' answer would be surprising to both Jews and Samaritans: location is not important. Rather, God requires his people to worship "in the Spirit and in truth" (v. 24). Thus, Jesus implicitly brings the conversation back to the living water of which he previously spoke.

When Jesus tells the woman that he is the Messiah that both Jews and Samaritans are waiting for, she no longer avoids the townspeople. Rather, she is so excited by her discovery that she boldly shares her story and leads the villagers to Jesus. They initially believe in Jesus because of her testimony (v. 39). After hearing Jesus for themselves, they are even more convinced. These villagers received salvation because the pariah had the courage to preach.

1. Who are the biggest social outcasts in today's culture? In what ways do religious rules sometimes marginalize these people?

2. When the Samaritan woman felt shame, she picked a fight. In what ways do you sometimes put up barriers when others are trying to help you?

3. Why do you think the Samaritan woman changed from being defensive to accepting the truth of who Jesus is?

TWO

Women at the Empty Tomb

John 20:11–18 ESV *But Mary stood weeping outside the tomb, and as she wept she stooped to look into the tomb. [12]And she saw two angels in white, sitting where the body of Jesus had lain, one at the head and one at the feet. [13]They said to her, "Woman, why are you weeping?" She said to them, "They have taken away my Lord, and I do not know where they have laid him." [14]Having said this, she turned around and saw Jesus standing, but she did not know that it was Jesus. [15]Jesus said to her, "Woman, why are you weeping? Whom are you seeking?" Supposing him to be the gardener, she said to him, "Sir, if you have carried him away, tell me where you have laid him, and I will take him away." [16]Jesus said to her, "Mary." She turned and said to him in Aramaic, "Rabboni!" (which means Teacher). [17]Jesus said to her, "Do not cling to me, for I have not yet ascended to the Father; but go to my brothers and say to them, 'I am ascending to my Father and your Father, to my God and your God.'" [18]Mary Magdalene went and announced to the disciples, "I have seen the Lord"—and that he had said these things to her.*

Read also Matthew 28:1–10; Mark 16:1–11; and Luke 24:1–12.

Key Observation. Christ often chooses unexpected people to serve as his witnesses.

Understanding the Word. All four Gospels agree that women are the first witnesses of the empty tomb and the first to proclaim the good news that Jesus is alive. They receive a supernatural commission to do so.

Several women rose early to go to the tomb. Although their names differ in the Gospels, all four accounts agree that Mary Magdalene is a central figure. She is so important that John telescopes his story to focus solely on her perspective. Earlier in Jesus' ministry we learned that she is one of the women who traveled with Jesus and provided for him out of her own means. It's no wonder: Jesus had cast out seven demons from her (see Luke 8:1–3). Mary is also one of the few disciples who witnessed Jesus' death and saw where he was buried (see Matthew 27:55–56, 61; Mark 15:40–41, 47; John 19:25).

Although Joseph of Arimathea and Nicodemus had performed the burial rite a few days earlier, the women leave for the tomb as soon as possible on the first day of the week. They had faithfully observed the Sabbath, but now they could get back to work. Even though there is no need to add more spices to the tomb, these grieving women want to offer one last act of devotion to Jesus.

Matthew's Gospel adds ironic humor to the story. The big, burly Roman soldiers are so afraid of the angel that they faint, but these ordinary women are bold enough to speak with the powerful angel. He shows the women the empty tomb, reminds them that Jesus predicted this would occur, and commands them to spread the good news to the disciples. After faithfully setting out to find the disciples, the women encounter the risen Christ. Jesus himself then commissions them to preach the good news.

John's Gospel focuses the story more tightly around Mary Magdalene. Here we see Mary's confusion at the empty tomb. Angels ask why she is crying, hinting at the joy she will soon experience. The body has not been stolen; something far greater has occurred. Then Mary sees Jesus, but she doesn't recognize him. Something about the resurrection body is different enough to cause this confusion (see also Luke 24:13–35). In a beautiful literary allusion, Mary finally recognizes Jesus when he calls her by name. Thus, Jesus' proclamation in John 10 comes true: the sheep know the voice of the Good Shepherd, who calls them by name and lays down his life for them. Jesus then tells Mary that she can't hold on to this reunion moment, because much is about to change. He soon will ascend to the Father, and so she must go and spread the news to the other disciples.

In a culture where women were not considered credible witnesses, Jesus once again demonstrates that God turns the values of the world upside down. The "weak" and "foolish" are now powerful proclaimers of the gospel.

1. In their grief, the women forgot Jesus' prediction of the resurrection. When have you been so overcome by emotion that you forgot God's promises? What later caused you to remember them?

2. In today's society, whose witness do we tend to ignore? Why?

3. What made these women powerful witnesses of the gospel?

THREE

Phoebe

Romans 16:1–2 *I commend to you our sister Phoebe, a deacon of the church at Cenchreae, ²so that you may welcome her in the Lord as is fitting for the saints, and help her in whatever she may require from you, for she has been a benefactor of many and of myself as well.*

Key Observation. Paul affirmed both men and women as leaders in the church.

Understanding the Word. The apostle Paul is staying in Corinth at the end of his third missionary journey when he writes his lengthy letter to the Romans. In order to deliver his letter, he will send it with Phoebe, a wealthy woman from nearby Cenchreae. She is probably a Gentile Christian, since her name has Greek mythological roots.

Paul commends Phoebe to the Roman churches. Traveling church leaders often carried letters of recommendation to ease their transition from one place to another. Paul refers to Phoebe as "our sister," just as he had earlier referred to Timothy as "our brother" and coworker (see 1 Thessalonians 3:2). Paul then describes Phoebe's position as a deacon in the church. This word can also mean minister or servant. Elsewhere in his letters Paul uses the term to refer to himself (see 1 Corinthians 3:5; 2 Corinthians 6:4; Ephesians 3:7; Colossians 1:23, 25) and other leaders in the early churches (see 1 Corinthians 3:5; Ephesians 6:21; Colossians 4:7). Epaphras, for example, preached the gospel to the Colossians. Paul calls him a "faithful minister [deacon] of Christ" on Paul's behalf (Col. 1:7). Phoebe is in good company.

Not only is she a key leader in the church, but she is also a patron ("benefactor") of the church. In the ancient world, patrons were wealthy and socially influential leaders who supported various causes. Since Paul does not connect Phoebe to a male head of household, she is likely a widow or divorcee who has significant social standing in her community. It appears she has financially supported both Paul and numerous others in the Christian churches. She is the kind of person who has connections. Thus, it is in the best interest of the Romans to befriend her.

But Phoebe is more than an influential woman. She is also a trusted emissary. Paul charges Phoebe with delivering his important communication. In the ancient world, it was customary for the person who delivered the letter to stand in for the person who wrote the letter. Thus, Phoebe likely reads the letter to the Romans and answers on Paul's behalf any questions raised by the Roman Christians. What a great privilege and great responsibility!

Although Phoebe is the first female deacon in the early church, she is not the last. In the first few centuries of the Christian church, numerous women are called deacon or deaconess in writings and tombstone inscriptions. As Greco-Roman thought influenced the church, many male church leaders tried to quash the involvement of these women, believing them to be weak and inferior. Scripture itself, however, testifies to the vital ministry of female leaders in the church.

1. Phoebe is called *sister*, *deacon*, and *benefactor*. How does each title place a different emphasis on Phoebe's personality?

2. Since Phoebe would read Paul's letter to the Roman churches and answer any questions about it, what does this say about Phoebe's education level and understanding of the gospel?

3. In what ways have you witnessed gender divisions in your church? Do both men and women serve in all roles? Why or why not?

FOUR

Priscilla

Acts 18:1–3, 18a–19, 24–26 *After this Paul left Athens and went to Corinth.*
²There he found a Jew named Aquila, a native of Pontus, who had recently come
from Italy with his wife Priscilla, because Claudius had ordered all Jews to leave
Rome. Paul went to see them, ³and, because he was of the same trade, he stayed
with them, and they worked together—by trade they were tentmakers. . . .

¹⁸After staying there for a considerable time, Paul said farewell to the believers
and sailed for Syria, accompanied by Priscilla and Aquila. . . . ¹⁹When they
reached Ephesus, he left them there, but first he himself went into the synagogue
and had a discussion with the Jews. . . .

²⁴Now there came to Ephesus a Jew named Apollos, a native of Alexandria.
He was an eloquent man, well-versed in the scriptures. ²⁵He had been instructed
in the Way of the Lord; and he spoke with burning enthusiasm and taught accu-
rately the things concerning Jesus, though he knew only the baptism of John. ²⁶He
began to speak boldly in the synagogue; but when Priscilla and Aquila heard
him, they took him aside and explained the Way of God to him more accurately.

Romans 16:3–5a *Greet Prisca and Aquila, who work with me in Christ Jesus,*
⁴and who risked their necks for my life, to whom not only I give thanks, but also
all the churches of the Gentiles. ⁵Greet also the church in their house.

Read also 1 Corinthians 16:19 and 2 Timothy 4:19.

Key Observation. Husbands and wives together can become great teams for
preaching the gospel.

Understanding the Word. Scripture connects Priscilla (also known as
Prisca) and her husband, Aquila, to churches in Corinth, Ephesus, and Rome.
They first become acquainted with Paul when he arrives in Corinth. They hit it
off immediately, finding a connection in their mutual work as tentmakers. Paul
and Aquila also have their Jewish heritage in common; Scripture does not tell
us whether Priscilla is a Jew or a Gentile.

As they sit making tents, they probably discuss the reason for Priscilla and Aquila's recent move from Rome to Corinth. In 49 CE, Emperor Claudius forced many Jews to leave Rome because they were arguing with one another over whether Jesus was the promised Messiah. Claudius was fed up with the uproar.

Such riots are not surprising to Paul, who has experienced many of his own. In fact, the longer he stays in Corinth, the more the non-Christian Jews get riled up. But the proconsul of the city, Gallio, refuses to intervene. After a year and a half, Paul is ready to move on to other cities. He convinces Priscilla and Aquila to join him in the work of planting churches. When they all stop in Ephesus, Paul leaves the couple there to continue their evangelism while he moves on to other locales. Despite working as tentmakers, Priscilla and Aquila are relatively wealthy. Their large home provides enough space for the church to meet there.

As they continue their work in Ephesus, the couple discover that a Jew from Alexandria, Egypt, has started preaching about Jesus. Alexandria was a great center of learning, and Apollos clearly has benefitted from his education there. He knows the Jewish Scriptures backward and forward and he is convinced that they testify about Jesus. Apollos zealously preaches about Christ in the synagogue, but he has not learned everything he needs to know about the gospel. Priscilla and Aquila gently take him aside and privately teach him more fully about the gospel message, especially baptism. Clearly, Priscilla's role in the church includes teaching.

It is important to note that four of the six times Priscilla and Aquila are mentioned in the New Testament, Priscilla's name is listed first. This suggests she has greater social status or is more involved in church ministry than her husband.

After Emperor Claudius dies in 54 CE, Priscilla and Aquila move back to Rome, now that it is safe to do so. When Paul writes to the Roman churches, he includes a greeting to the couple. He calls them coworkers in Christ, a term he uses for other key church leaders, including Titus, Timothy, Philemon, and Luke. It appears that Priscilla and Aquila, like Phoebe, had served as patrons of Paul. He makes it clear that they have taken some risk in order to defend him. Whatever their intervention, the other churches applaud the actions of these selfless leaders.

1. Priscilla and Aquila used whatever circumstances in which they found themselves (whether refugees, artisans, or patrons) to preach the gospel. What opportunities do you have to share the gospel in your own spheres of influence?

2. Priscilla and Aquila were not heavy-handed when they corrected Apollos. How can we follow their model when correcting others?

3. In what ways can a ministry team sometimes be more effective than an individual?

FIVE

Junia

Romans 16:7 NIV *Greet Andronicus and Junia, my fellow Jews who have been in prison with me.*

They are outstanding among the apostles, and they were in Christ before I was.

Key Observation. Some great leaders are not well recognized.

Understanding the Word. As Paul finishes writing Romans, he offers a list of greetings to many believers he knows in Rome. (Remarkably, nine of the twenty-six individuals are women.) Paul has not yet visited Rome, but he wants to show his many connections. He hopes that this will help the Roman churches to trust his gospel wisdom.

Although some commentators suggest "Junia" is a form of the male "Junianus," historical evidence points to a female name. No examples of the male form exist in this time period, but more than 250 uses of the female name occur. In addition, the earliest church fathers affirm that Junia is a woman.

Thus, Andronicus and Junia are likely husband and wife. Despite the Greco-Roman names, they are Jews like Paul. (Keep in mind that "Paul" is Saul's Greco-Roman name.) At some point, they were imprisoned with Paul for preaching the gospel, but it is difficult to identify which imprisonment. Paul holds the couple in high esteem, noting they have known Christ longer than he has.

The most striking aspect of this greeting is that Paul calls them "outstanding among the apostles." Some interpreters have suggested that the phrase means they are well-known to the apostles. The most direct reading of the Greek, however, suggests that the couple are apostles themselves. Not only this, but they are considered *outstanding examples* of apostles. Clearly they are not part of the twelve apostles of Jesus, but the New Testament uses the term *apostle* in several ways. It can also refer to those disciples who witnessed the risen Christ, and it can refer to disciples who are sent out to accomplish a specific ministry. Either way, Andronicus and Junia are key leaders in the early church, witnessing to the power of Christ.

It may seem odd that we have not heard more about Andronicus and Junia if they truly are apostles. But we may know more than we think. Junia is likely another name for Joanna, a woman whom Jesus had healed. She traveled with Jesus and helped to provide for him financially (see Luke 8:3). She had the means to do this because her husband, Chuza, worked as a steward for King Herod. The Greco-Roman name "Junia" would have served Joanna well in that political context. Similarly, "Andronicus" may be the Greco-Roman name for Chuza. (Another possibility is that Chuza died and later Joanna married Andronicus.) Most importantly, Joanna is one of the women who witnessed the empty tomb (see Luke 24:10).

Andronicus and Junia are well-known leaders within the early church. By the fourth century, John Chrysostom comments: "To be an apostle is something great! But to be outstanding among the apostles—just think what a wonderful song of praise that is! They were outstanding on the basis of their works and virtuous actions. Indeed, how great the wisdom of this woman must have been that she was even deemed worthy of the title of apostle." Over time, Junia's story was lost in history, but Paul's simple greeting reminds us of her contribution to the early church.

1. How did Junia's earlier experiences of Jesus prepare her for the later difficulties of ministry?

2. What might make an apostle appear outstanding in the eyes of other apostles?

3. Who do you know who works tirelessly for the gospel without receiving applause? How can you encourage them this week?

WEEK FOUR

GATHERING DISCUSSION OUTLINE

A. **Open session in prayer.** Ask that God would astonish us anew with fresh insight from God's Word and transform us into the disciples that Jesus desires us to become.

B. **View video for this week's readings.**

C. **What were key insights or takeaways that you gained from your reading during the week and from watching the video commentary?** In particular, how did these help you to grow in your faith and understanding of Scripture this week? What parts of the Bible lesson or study raised questions for you?

D. **Discuss selected questions from the daily readings.** Invite class members to share key insights or to raise questions that they found to be the most meaningful.

1. **KEY OBSERVATION:** Meeting Christ transforms people.

   DISCUSSION QUESTION: Why do you think the Samaritan woman changed from being defensive to accepting the truth of who Jesus is?

2. **KEY OBSERVATION:** Christ often chooses unexpected people to serve as his witnesses.

   DISCUSSION QUESTION: What made these women powerful witnesses of the gospel?

3. **KEY OBSERVATION:** Paul affirmed both men and women as leaders in the church.

   DISCUSSION QUESTION: In what ways have you witnessed gender divisions in your church? Do both men and women serve in all roles? Why or why not?

4. **KEY OBSERVATION:** Husbands and wives together can become great teams for preaching the gospel.

   DISCUSSION QUESTION: In what ways can a ministry team sometimes be more effective than an individual?

5. **KEY OBSERVATION:** Some great leaders are not well recognized.

   DISCUSSION QUESTION: Who do you know who works tirelessly for the gospel without receiving applause? How can you encourage them this week?

E. **As the study concludes, consider specific ways that this week's Bible lessons invite you to grow and call you to change.** How do they call us to think differently? How do they challenge us to change in order to align ourselves with God's work in the world? What specific actions should we take to apply the insights of the lesson into our daily lives? What kind of person does our Bible lesson call us to become?

F. **Close session with prayer.** Emphasize God's ongoing work of transformation in our lives in preparation for loving mission and service in the world. Pray for absent class members as well as for persons whom we need to invite to join our study.

WEEK FIVE

The Context of Female Leadership in the Church

ONE

Headship and Head Coverings in Corinth (Part One)

1 Corinthians 11:3–15a ESV *But I want you to understand that the head of every man is Christ, the head of a wife is her husband, and the head of Christ is God. ⁴Every man who prays or prophesies with his head covered dishonors his head, ⁵but every wife who prays or prophesies with her head uncovered dishonors her head, since it is the same as if her head were shaven. ⁶For if a wife will not cover her head, then she should cut her hair short. But since it is disgraceful for a wife to cut off her hair or shave her head, let her cover her head. ⁷For a man ought not to cover his head, since he is the image and glory of God, but woman is the glory of man. ⁸For man was not made from woman, but woman from man. ⁹Neither was man created for woman, but woman for man. ¹⁰That is why a wife ought to have a symbol of authority on her head, because of the angels. ¹¹Nevertheless, in the Lord woman is not independent of man nor man of woman; ¹²for as woman was made from man, so man is now born of woman. And all things are from God. ¹³Judge for yourselves: is it proper for a wife to pray to God with her head uncovered? ¹⁴Does not nature itself teach you that if a man wears long hair it is a disgrace for him, ¹⁵but if a woman has long hair, it is her glory?*

Key Observation. Freedom in Christ must be balanced with restraint.

Understanding the Word. This week's studies explore passages in which a surface reading does not give the whole picture. Readers need to understand the situation in Paul's churches before drawing conclusions about the text's meaning. Today's reading comes from a section where Paul is advising the Corinthian church on proper worship practices. As he makes clear throughout chapters 11 to 14, worship should be orderly. Individuals should not distract attention away from God.

In 11:2–16, the distraction comes in the form of wives who have uncovered their heads while praying and prophesying in church. This is an important starting point: women are taking public roles in worship services in Corinth. As we saw last week, Paul affirms female ministers of the gospel. Thus, the issue here is not *whether* women should speak, but the *manner* in which they speak.

In order to understand Paul's concern, we must explore the cultural expectations of Paul's day. In that honor–shame culture, it was extremely important to protect the honor of one's family through one's actions. Respectable women wore their hair tied back or under a veil. Wearing hair loose often meant that one was a loose woman. In some of the pagan temples in Corinth, temple prostitutes wore their hair flowing loose when they had ecstatic visions. If a woman wore her hair short or shorn, it had shameful implications. In the Jewish world, for example, a convicted adulteress would be forced to shave her head. In Greco-Roman circles, very short hair on a woman might indicate she was a lesbian. Similarly, men who wore long hair indicated they were homosexual. In first-century Corinth, much more than in twenty-first-century Western culture, hairstyles made statements about identity.

Although Paul has argued for freedom in Christ, believers still live in a culture where that freedom can be misinterpreted. This section of his letter reminds believers that their freedom must be lived with restraint. If freedom distracts others from the gospel, then it should be curtailed out of love for one's brother or sister in Christ (see also 1 Corinthians 8:9–13). Wives who are publicly speaking in worship should appear modest in their behavior and customs. If a woman's hairstyle leads others to think she is a lesbian or promiscuous, then she is not demonstrating fidelity to her husband. He is dishonored.

This is why Paul includes language about the wife being the glory of her husband (v. 7). Paul identifies the man as both the image and glory of God.

Like Adam, the man was created in God's image and is, in essence, part of God's family. He should bring glory (honor) to that family. A woman (who is also made in the image of God) leaves her own family and marries into a new one. Thus, she should bring glory (honor) to her new family. If she were to let her hair flow loose in worship, it would be similar to a married woman today taking off her wedding ring in public. A certain disloyalty is implied.

1. What does your wardrobe and lifestyle communicate to others about your own identity?

2. What are some ways we might be tempted to be free in Christ, but which might give others the wrong impression?

3. How can we know where the line is between expressing freedom and unintentionally harming our brother or sister in Christ?

TWO

Headship and Head Coverings in Corinth (Part Two)

1 Corinthians 11:3–15a ESV *But I want you to understand that the head of every man is Christ, the head of a wife is her husband, and the head of Christ is God. ⁴Every man who prays or prophesies with his head covered dishonors his head, ⁵but every wife who prays or prophesies with her head uncovered dishonors her head, since it is the same as if her head were shaven. ⁶For if a wife will not cover her head, then she should cut her hair short. But since it is disgraceful for a wife to cut off her hair or shave her head, let her cover her head. ⁷For a man ought not to cover his head, since he is the image and glory of God, but woman is the glory of man. ⁸For man was not made from woman, but woman from man. ⁹Neither was man created for woman, but woman for man. ¹⁰That is why a wife ought to have a symbol of authority on her head, because of the angels. ¹¹Nevertheless, in the Lord woman is not independent of man nor man of woman; ¹²for as woman was made from man, so man is now born of woman. And all things are from God. ¹³Judge for yourselves: is it proper for a wife to pray to God with her head uncovered? ¹⁴Does not nature itself teach you* *that if a man wears long hair it is a disgrace for him, ¹⁵but if a woman has long hair, it is her glory?*

Key Observation. Men and women are not independent of one another, but interdependent.

Understanding the Word. One of the more difficult issues in this passage concerns the idea of headship. What does it mean that the husband is the "head" of his wife? Is there a God-ordained hierarchy within a marriage? Certainly, the culture in which Paul lived was extremely patriarchal. The husband was the head of the household and ultimate authority in both Jewish and Greco-Roman homes.

But Paul understands that life in Christ radically reorders relationships. Whereas the world defines a person by their wealth, social status, gender, and ethnicity, God defines a person by their commitment to Christ. The typical status markers of that culture mean nothing to the God who "does not show favoritism" (Rom. 2:11 NIV).

On the surface, verse 3 seems to imply a hierarchy. Notice, however, the order of the statements. If Paul wanted to lay out a strict hierarchy of relationships, he would order the list from top to bottom: God/Christ, Christ/man, man/woman. But instead, Paul intentionally mis-orders the pairs. This signals that he intends a different reading.

In addition, the term *head* had multiple meanings in the ancient world. Most often it meant a physical head, just as it frequently does here in 1 Corinthians. Sometimes Paul uses this term metaphorically. When used this way, the term can imply authority or describe a *source*. (For example, the "head" of a river is its source). In verse 10, Paul uses the word *authority* rather than head. Specifically, Paul says that "because of the angels" wives should have "authority" on their heads. The most likely explanation for this cryptic reference involves the Jewish belief that angels were present during worship and watched over creation order. They would be offended if a wife dishonored her husband. A modest symbol of marital fidelity (a veil or hair pulled back) is in order.

After addressing the specific situation of the angels, Paul emphasizes the interdependence of man and woman. Although woman originated from man (i.e., Eve came from Adam's rib), men now are born through women. Yet "all things are from God" (v. 12). This brings us back to the pairings of verse 3, where Paul is emphasizing the source of all life. Christ, with God, created all humanity. Adam was the source of Eve. But all things come through Christ, who in his incarnation came from God. Men and women are not independent from one another, but interdependent. Mutuality is the key value here, not dominance or hierarchy.

Thus, Paul uses headship language to urge women to lead in worship in an orderly way that shows respect for their marriage. The manner in which this respect is displayed will differ from culture to culture (e.g., head coverings in most Western cultures no longer indicate such respect), but the principle remains the same.

1. Does your culture focus more on the independence or interdependence of men and women? In what ways?

2. What are some ways that husbands and wives today publicly show respect for one another?

3. How can the church work harder at honoring both husbands and wives as they serve the kingdom?

THREE

Silence in the Church

1 Corinthians 14:34–35 NIV *Women should remain silent in the churches. They are not allowed to speak, but must be in submission, as the law says. ³⁵If they want to inquire about something, they should ask their own husbands at home; for it is disgraceful for a woman to speak in the church.*

Key Observation. Worship should be orderly and respectful.

Understanding the Word. This brief passage, inserted within a section on prophets speaking in the church, stands in stark contrast to 1 Corinthians 11. There, Paul instructs wives regarding praying and prophesying in church. Here, it appears he silences women. Either Paul is unaware of the contradiction (which is highly unlikely), or something else is happening in Corinth that Paul needs to address.

Several clues aid the interpretation of this passage. First, the word used for *women* can also mean *wives*. This narrows the scope of the command and addresses some kind of marital issue. The second clue lies in verse 35, where Paul gives more context: "If they want to inquire about something, they should ask their husbands at home." This suggests that the women are asking questions *during* the worship service. In other words, they are disrupting worship with their questions. This idea is reinforced by the Greek word used for *speak*, which can also mean "babble" or "chatter." The wives are chattering in the middle of worship. Women in the ancient world generally received much less education than men; it would be understandable for wives to ask their husbands for clarification of the teaching. Since these churches met in homes rather than synagogues or other public meeting spaces, the meeting may have felt more like domestic space than sacred space. The restraint that a person might normally feel in a public meeting is lessened when one meets in a more intimate setting. This confusion may help us understand why Paul says it is "disgraceful" for a wife to speak in church. A home is a perfectly appropriate place for wives to ask questions of their husbands. When the house is being used as a church, however, the leader must be allowed to speak without side conversations disrupting the service.

One curious aspect of this passage is Paul's comment that the law commands women to "be in submission" (literally, "submit themselves"). Nothing in the Old Testament contains this requirement. Paul may be referring to a more general principle in Scripture. That is, he urges these wives to be humble learners rather than aggressive interrogators. Scripture often speaks of the position of the student as one of humble learning (e.g., Proverbs 1:5; Psalm 25:8–9). Notice that the command to "be in submission" requires *internal* restraint. It is not a subjection imposed by others. Thus, Paul is not prohibiting women from speaking or learning (or even asking questions), but instead he focuses on the *manner* in which these activities occur.

All of chapters 11–14 focus on orderly worship, and 14:34–35 provides no exception. Even in 14:33, where Paul addresses prophecies in the church, he comments that God is not a God "of disorder, but of peace." In 14:34–35, Paul is irritated that people (in this case, wives) are interrupting worship. He wishes to restore order by urging wives to withhold their questions until a more appropriate time.

1. What interruptions sometimes occur during worship? How does this affect a person's ability to focus on the message?

2. In what ways can believers take the position of a humble learner?

3. In what ways can your church develop an orderly atmosphere that helps people focus on the gospel message?

FOUR
Women in the Ephesian Church (Part One)

1 Timothy 2:8–15 *I desire, then, that in every place the men should pray, lifting up holy hands without anger or argument; ⁹also that the women should dress themselves modestly and decently in suitable clothing, not with their hair braided, or with gold, pearls, or expensive clothes, ¹⁰but with good works, as is proper for women who profess reverence for God. ¹¹Let a woman learn in silence with full submission. ¹²I permit no woman to teach or to have authority over a man; she is to keep silent. ¹³For Adam was formed first, then Eve; ¹⁴and Adam was not deceived, but the woman was deceived and became a transgressor. ¹⁵Yet she will be saved through childbearing, provided they continue in faith and love and holiness, with modesty.*

Key Observation. Anyone who promotes a false doctrine should be prohibited from teaching until they learn the basics of the gospel.

Understanding the Word. The beginning of this passage echoes themes found in 1 Corinthians 11 and 14. Modesty is an important virtue, even though the letter to Timothy does not mention head coverings while prophesying. Braided hair, however, does merit a comment. During this time period, intricately braided hairstyles came to be markers of status. Believers in the Ephesian church, however, learn that they should avoid showy dress and ostentatious hairstyles. Rather, Christians should be known for their good works.

In order to understand the commands in verses 11–15, one needs to consider carefully the religious context of Ephesus, where Timothy is serving as pastor. (Many scholars consider this letter to be written in Paul's name by one of his later disciples. Either way, the author presumes an Ephesian context.) The city was a hotbed of magic and religion. Tourists flocked to Ephesus to see the Temple of Artemis, one of the seven wonders of the ancient world. The goddess Artemis was the patron deity of the city. In other words, residents believed she protected them and caused their lives to prosper. Ephesian Artemis was the goddess of fertility and childbirth. Many of the priests in the temple were women. In addition, legend held that Amazon women had once taken refuge in the city. Thus, Ephesus had a tradition of influential women in positions of authority.

It would be natural for converts to Christianity to think that worship in the Christian church would be similar to worship in the pagan cults elsewhere in the city. Both letters to Timothy demonstrate significant concern that false teaching is present in the Ephesian church (see 1 Timothy 1:3–4, 19–20; 6:3–5; 2 Timothy 2:17–18; 3:6–9). In fact, 2 Timothy 3:6–7 indicates that the false teaching has especially influenced some of the women in the church. This helps us to understand the command in 1 Timothy 2:11 that women should "learn in silence and with full submission." They need to learn the truth of the gospel before they are allowed to teach. The phrasing in verse 12 is in the present tense, which can translate, "I am not currently permitting." The prohibition against women teaching is likely a temporary one. Furthermore, the Greek word for "have authority" is not the usual term for such a command. Rather, this unusual word has the connotation of "grasping at authority" or "domineering." It appears that Timothy is struggling with Ephesian women who are trying to dominate the church with their false doctrine. The prohibition thus refers to this specific behavior. Once again, the *manner* of speaking in church is the issue, not the speaking itself.

1. What does modesty look like in today's culture? When does wealth cross over into showing off?

2. What kinds of false gospels sometimes creep into the church today?

3. Under what conditions might you temporarily prohibit someone from speaking in church?

FIVE

Women in the Ephesian Church (Part Two)

1 Timothy 2:8–15 *I desire, then, that in every place the men should pray, lifting up holy hands without anger or argument; ⁹also that the women should dress themselves modestly and decently in suitable clothing, not with their hair braided, or with gold, pearls, or expensive clothes, ¹⁰but with good works, as is proper for women who profess reverence for God. ¹¹Let a woman learn in silence with full submission. ¹²I permit no woman to teach or to have authority over a man; she is to keep silent. ¹³For Adam was formed first, then Eve; ¹⁴and Adam was not deceived, but the woman was deceived and became a transgressor. ¹⁵Yet she will be saved through childbearing, provided they continue in faith and love and holiness, with modesty.*

Key Observation. Understanding the context of the first-century churches is crucial for interpretation.

Understanding the Word. On the surface, creation theology appears to support the prohibition against women teaching and having authority in the Ephesian church. Verse 13 clarifies that Adam was created prior to Eve, while verse 14 explains that the first person to be deceived by the serpent was Eve. Yet these statements sound odd compared to what Paul says elsewhere in his letters. As we saw in 1 Corinthians 11, Paul emphasizes that even though woman came from man (i.e., Adam was created first), ever since then, every man comes from a woman. Paul highlights the interdependence of man and woman (vv. 8, 11–12). Yet here, Adam's priority in creation is underscored. Furthermore, elsewhere Paul writes about Adam—not Eve—as the transgressor (e.g., Romans 5:12–19; 1 Corinthians 15:21–22). So why the different focus here?

Once again, the false teaching in Ephesus helps us to understand this passage. Greco-Roman religions often borrowed themes from other religions and shaped them into new ideas. It appears that early Gnostics did this with the creation narratives in Genesis. Although Gnosticism takes a variety of forms, some versions describe Eve as being created prior to Adam. In these traditions, she was his superior and taught him eternal truths. If these myths were part of the superstitions in Ephesus, then it is easy to understand why the letter to Timothy emphasizes creation order. It is correcting false teaching.

The final verse in this section also responds to false teaching. The idea of being "saved through childbearing" sounds very unlike Paul, who regularly proclaims that salvation occurs through faith alone (see Romans 3:28; 4:5; 10:9; Galatians 2:16; 3:11; Ephesians 2:8–9; Titus 3:5). But 1 Timothy 4:3 gives us a clue as to why the question of childbearing is pertinent in Ephesus: some false teachers are forbidding marriage. This teaching may also be linked to early Gnostic ideas. One of the basic beliefs of Gnosticism was that the physical realm was imperfect; only the spiritual would live on. For some Gnostics, the focus on the spiritual led them to abandon any physical entanglements in this world; thus, marriage and childbirth should be avoided if one wants to achieve salvation. The letter to Timothy may be correcting this twisted theology, reassuring women that salvation is indeed possible for those who participate in the physicality of marriage and childbirth.

Another plausible interpretation of verse 15 focuses on very specific language: the Greek says she will be saved through "the" childbearing. If Eve is still the focus here, then the warning to the serpent in Genesis 3:15 may be in view: Eve's offspring will crush the serpent's head. This was fulfilled in Christ, who crushed sin and death through his sacrifice on the cross. Thus, Ephesians who rely on Artemis to save them through childbirth must realize that true salvation only comes through a life dedicated to Jesus Christ.

1. What are ways that you can prepare yourself to recognize false teaching in the church?

2. What modern examples can you think of that show how messages can be misinterpreted when the larger context is ignored?

3. How does comparing the various writings of Paul help when interpreting difficult passages in Paul's letters?

WEEK FIVE

GATHERING DISCUSSION OUTLINE

A. **Open session in prayer.** Ask that God would astonish us anew with fresh insight from God's Word and transform us into the disciples that Jesus desires us to become.

B. **View video for this week's readings.**

C. **What were key insights or takeaways that you gained from your reading during the week and from watching the video commentary?** In particular, how did these help you to grow in your faith and understanding of Scripture this week? What parts of the Bible lessons or study raised questions for you?

D. **Discuss selected questions from the daily readings.** Invite class members to share key insights or to raise questions that they found to be the most meaningful.

1. **KEY OBSERVATION:** Freedom in Christ must be balanced with restraint.

    DISCUSSION QUESTION: How can we know where the line is between expressing freedom and unintentionally harming our brother or sister in Christ?

2. **KEY OBSERVATION:** Men and women are not independent of one another, but interdependent.

    DISCUSSION QUESTION: How can the church work harder at honoring both husbands and wives as they serve the kingdom?

3. **KEY OBSERVATION:** Worship should be orderly and respectful.

    DISCUSSION QUESTION: In what ways can your church develop an orderly atmosphere that helps people focus on the gospel message?

4. **KEY OBSERVATION:** Anyone who promotes a false doctrine should be prohibited from teaching until they learn the basics of the gospel.

    DISCUSSION QUESTION: Under what conditions might you temporarily prohibit someone from speaking in church?

5. **KEY OBSERVATION:** Understanding the context of the first-century churches is crucial for interpretation.

    DISCUSSION QUESTION: What modern examples can you think of that show how messages can be misinterpreted when the larger context is ignored?

E. **As the study concludes, consider specific ways that this week's Bible lessons invite you to grow and call you to change.** How do they call us to think differently? How do they challenge us to change in order to align ourselves with God's work in the world? What specific actions should we take to apply the insights of the lessons into our daily lives? What kind of person do our Bible lessons call us to become?

F. **Close session with prayer.** Emphasize God's ongoing work of transformation in our lives in preparation for loving mission and service in the world. Pray for absent class members as well as for persons whom we need to invite to join our study.

The Role of Women in the Household

ONE

Household Codes in Ephesus (Part One)

Ephesians 5:21–33 *Be subject to one another out of reverence for Christ.*
[22]Wives, be subject to your husbands as you are to the Lord. [23]For the husband is the head of the wife just as Christ is the head of the church, the body of which he is the Savior. [24]Just as the church is subject to Christ, so also wives ought to be, in everything, to their husbands.

[25]Husbands, love your wives, just as Christ loved the church and gave himself up for her, [26]in order to make her holy by cleansing her with the washing of water by the word, [27]so as to present the church to himself in splendor, without a spot or wrinkle or anything of the kind—yes, so that she may be holy and without blemish. [28]In the same way, husbands should love their wives as they do their own bodies. He who loves his wife loves himself. [29]For no one ever hates his own body, but he nourishes and tenderly cares for it, just as Christ does for the church, [30]because we are members of his body. [31]"For this reason a man will leave his father and mother and be joined to his wife, and the two will become one flesh." [32]This is a great mystery, and I am applying it to Christ and the church. [33]Each of you, however, should love his wife as himself, and a wife should respect her husband.

Key Observation. Christ is the source of love that empowers us to submit to one another.

Understanding the Word. Does the role of women in the home differ from that of women in the church? Last week we considered public roles of women; this week we will explore the roles of women within their families.

An interesting fact about Scripture is that the earliest manuscripts contain no paragraphs (or chapter and verse markers). Only centuries later did editors suggest where blocks of thought started and ended. So if you look at different translations of Scripture, you will find that subject headings occur in different spots. In Ephesians 5, some versions place verse 21 with the preceding paragraph. The New Revised Standard Version, however, correctly begins the new section with verse 21. It serves as a theme verse for everything that follows. The relationship between husbands and wives, parents and children, masters and slaves, all provide examples of mutual submission. Yet the command to submit to one another is given to *all* believers to follow. "Reverence for Christ" results in the desire to model our lives after Christ's own example of self-sacrifice. Mutual submission is based on selfless love.

This passage, like others we have explored, must be considered in light of the Greco-Roman context. The father held all of the power in the household. He determined the fate of his wife, children, and slaves. In a striking role reversal, Paul commands husbands to limit their culturally mandated power. In fact, Paul spends most of his time exhorting husbands to care for their wives. This was highly unusual for Paul's day!

Paul begins by addressing wives. They must be subject to (submit themselves to) their husbands. Paul's rationale is that the husband is the "head" of the wife, just as Christ is the "head" of the church. The last time Paul used this word in Ephesians, "source" was the primary meaning. In 4:15–16 he argued that the church body grows from infancy to maturity when it is connected to Christ. From Christ (literally, "out of" Christ) comes life and growth. Christ is the source. Here in chapter 5, the meaning is similar. A first-century husband was responsible for providing food and shelter for his wife. He is the source of her sustenance. Just as Christ provides for the life and growth of the church, so, too, does the first-century husband provide for the life and growth of his wife. The picture here is one of provision and growth, not authority or dominance.

When Paul tells the wife to submit to her husband in everything, he is not saying that she should obey her husband in all situations. In fact, the word "obey" never occurs in this passage! A woman's first duty is to follow God. If her husband asks her to do something against God's will, she must obey God and not her husband. Paul is asking, however, for a wife to act *as any believer should (including men)*—with patience, gentleness, humility, love, and peace (4:1–3). A peaceful home models mutual submission and the love of Christ.

1. How does the love of Christ provide a source for life and growth for you personally?

2. What are some concrete ways that a wife can lift up her husband in patience, gentleness, humility, love, and peace?

3. What are the best examples of mutual submission that you have seen?

TWO

Household Codes in Ephesus (Part Two)

Ephesians 5:21–33 *Be subject to one another out of reverence for Christ.*
²²Wives, be subject to your husbands as you are to the Lord. ²³For the husband is the head of the wife just as Christ is the head of the church, the body of which he is the Savior. ²⁴Just as the church is subject to Christ, so also wives ought to be, in everything, to their husbands.

²⁵Husbands, love your wives, just as Christ loved the church and gave himself up for her, ²⁶in order to make her holy by cleansing her with the washing of water by the word, ²⁷so as to present the church to himself in splendor, without a spot or wrinkle or anything of the kind—yes, so that she may be holy and without blemish. ²⁸In the same way, husbands should love their wives as they do their own bodies. He who loves his wife loves himself. ²⁹For no one ever hates his own body, but he nourishes and tenderly cares for it, just as Christ does for the church, ³⁰because we are members of his body. ³¹"For this reason a man will leave his father and mother and be joined to his wife, and the two will become one flesh." ³²This is a great mystery, and I am applying it to Christ and the church. ³³Each of you, however, should love his wife as himself, and a wife should respect her husband.

Key Observation. Paul asks husbands and wives to act as any believer should—with gentleness, humility, patience, peace, and sacrificial love.

Understanding the Word. Paul directs most of the instructions regarding mutual submission in marriage to the husbands. Despite a culture that told men they were in charge, Paul urges husbands to take a different approach. Six times he uses the word *love* in these instructions. In the Greco-Roman world, husbands were rarely told to love their wives. But that is Paul's focus here. The language is similar to 5:1–2, where Paul commands believers to "live in love, as Christ loved us and gave himself up for us." What Paul is asking, then, is for a husband to act *as any believer should (including women)*—with sacrificial love.

Verses 26–27 are quite unusual. Here Paul provides the image of a bride receiving a bath and clean clothes prior to her wedding. Yet drawing a bath and preparing bridal clothes were the tasks of women and slaves. Thus, Paul encourages the men, metaphorically, to do women's work. In other words, marriage is not about wielding culturally given authority. Rather, it involves a willingness to serve the other person and help them to be their best.

In a striking irony, Paul uses the self-centered principle of loving one's own body in order to explain how a husband should selflessly love his wife. People naturally care for themselves. They nourish, strengthen, and protect their bodies. It is important for a husband to see that his wife is not the "other," but rather, part of himself and part of his obligation to self-care. In order to support this logic, Paul turns to the creation narrative in Genesis. In marriage, the two become one flesh. The woman, as part of that one flesh, must be honored and taken care of, just as a man would take care of his own body. As Christ nourishes his body—the church—so, too, must a husband nourish and care for his own body (his wife).

In verse 33, Paul summarizes the discussion to this point: love and respect are necessary for mutual submission. Both husband and wife are asked to love their partner in a deeply sacrificial way. This relationship models the kind of self-giving love that all believers should have for one another.

1. What does our culture today tell men their roles should be in a marriage? How do Paul's instructions differ?

2. What are some concrete ways that a husband can love his wife as he loves his own body?

3. Consider the similarities between the fruit of the Spirit (see Galatians 5:22–23) and the characteristics found here in Ephesians. How would marriages look different if these commands were fully lived out?

THREE

True Beauty

1 Peter 3:1–7 NIV *Wives, in the same way submit yourselves to your own husbands so that, if any of them do not believe the word, they may be won over without words by the behavior of their wives, ²when they see the purity and reverence of your lives. ³Your beauty should not come from outward adornment, such as elaborate hairstyles and the wearing of gold jewelry or fine clothes. ⁴Rather, it should be that of your inner self, the unfading beauty of a gentle and quiet spirit, which is of great worth in God's sight. ⁵For this is the way the holy women of the past who put their hope in God used to adorn themselves. They submitted themselves to their own husbands, ⁶like Sarah, who obeyed Abraham and called him her lord. You are her daughters if you do what is right and do not give way to fear.*

⁷Husbands, in the same way be considerate as you live with your wives, and treat them with respect as the weaker partner and as heirs with you of the gracious gift of life, so that nothing will hinder your prayers.

Key Observation. Tension often exists between loyalty to Christ and loyalty to cultural expectations.

Understanding the Word. Peter's advice falls within a larger section addressing how Christians ought to behave when nonbelievers are watching. The good lives of believers serve as a testimony of the truth of the gospel. In chapter 3, Peter is addressing Christian wives whose husbands are nonbelievers. In the Greco-Roman world, the male head of household determined all things for the family, including religion. Thus, the Christian wife is already defying her husband by embracing Christianity. This may well have caused others in the community to question whether Christians were upsetting the order of society as a whole. Peter's advice to believers is to live such a good life that nonbelievers will have nothing but praise for God (2:12).

Not only should believing wives live pure and respectful lives (3:2), but they should avoid the competitive fashion statements that other Greco-Roman women made through dress, jewelry, and hairstyles. Instead, Peter explains that true beauty radiates from a person's inner spirit. (See similar themes in 1 Samuel 16:7 and Proverbs 31:30.) He gives the example of Sarah obeying

Abraham and calling him "lord." Although modern readers tend to think "lord" automatically means "God," it could also mean "master" or "sir." It was a term of respect. Thus, Peter is encouraging believing women to respect their husbands and, thus, create a peaceful household. They must not be intimidated by nonbelievers who might accuse them of wrongdoing. Rather, they should continue to follow Christ as well as honor their husbands.

When Peter addresses husbands, he carries over the advice he just gave to the wives. He tells husbands to treat their wives "in the same way" as he just directed the wives to act. In other words, gentleness and respect are qualities of Christians in general—without gender distinction. This does not mean that all gender differences are erased. Peter urges husbands to care for their wives as the "weaker partner." He is likely referring to the observation that, in general, women are not physically as strong as men. (This observation was heightened by the high mortality rate associated with childbirth.) Thus, a gentle spirit is even more important for men, who could easily overpower women.

Despite being physically weaker, women are heirs with their husbands when it comes to the inheritance of the kingdom. This mutuality is striking in a culture where inheritance was traced only through male lineage. Peter is reminding the husbands that even though physical differences exist between men and women, spiritual differences do not. Both are called to honor and respect one another, and those who are faithful will inherit eternal life.

1. In what ways do nonbelievers sometimes accuse Christians of wrongdoing?

2. How does Christlike behavior help to diffuse tensions with the surrounding culture?

3. Using Peter's definition of true beauty, who is the most beautiful person you know?

FOUR

The Testimony of Older Women

Titus 2:3–5 NIV *Likewise, teach the older women to be reverent in the way they live, not to be slanderers or addicted to much wine, but to teach what is good.*

⁴Then they can urge the younger women to love their husbands and children, ⁵to be self-controlled and pure, to be busy at home, to be kind, and to be subject to their husbands, so that no one will malign the word of God.

Key Observation. Living reverently involves recognizing that you are in God's presence and your life belongs to God.

Understanding the Word. False teaching is a concern in the letter to Titus, just as with the letters to Timothy. Titus, however, is pastoring on the island of Crete in the Mediterranean Sea. Here there is a rebellious circumcision group that is disrupting entire families (1:10–11). These false teachers are promoting certain Jewish traditions that contradict the gospel (1:14). Although these leaders claim to believe in Christ, they do not live a transformed life (1:16). In the ancient world, people from Crete had a reputation for dishonesty and laziness (1:12). It appears that these false teachers are not living any differently as Christians than they had lived before turning to Christ.

In contrast, the letter directs Titus to teach behaviors that agree with the "sound doctrine" of the gospel (2:1). Older men must be "temperate, worthy of respect, self-controlled, and sound in faith, in love and in endurance" (2:2 NIV). The instructions to the older women begin with "likewise," indicating that similar behavior is required regardless of gender. Just as older men are to be temperate and self-controlled, so, too, older women are to be reverent. The term used here for reverence literally means "what is proper for the temple." In other words, the older women should act in a way that recognizes they are in God's presence and that their very lives belong to God.

Two specific behaviors are prohibited, which suggests that older women in Crete struggled with these issues: slander and drunkenness. Some older women may have been overly critical of others, gossiping about them. Such negative language contradicts commands elsewhere to focus on building up the body of Christ (e.g., 1 Thessalonians 5:11; Romans 14:19; Ephesians 4:29; 1 Corinthians 14:26). Other women may have been heavy drinkers, literally "slaves" to wine (2:3). Titus must warn these women to avoid addictions that distract them from the gospel.

Instead, reverent women teach what is good and help younger women to live godly lives. Several examples then describe ways for young women to present a strong witness for the gospel. Since most women in the ancient world spent their energies in the domestic realm, these examples come from home life. (This does not mean these are the only activities in which a woman should participate.) Christian women must love their husband and children, be self-controlled (the same instruction given to older men in 2:2), pure, busy at home (in contrast to the "lazy" Cretans of 1:12), and kind. They must also be subject to their husbands (similar to Ephesians 5:22 and 1 Peter 3:1).

As we saw in yesterday's passage, the concern here is to live in such a godly way "that no one will malign the word of God" (v. 5, with the theme repeated in v. 8). False teachers are giving Christianity an ugly reputation. This letter addresses the issue by asking believers in Crete to live such godly lives that the gospel will be attractive to nonbelievers (2:10).

1. Why are slander and drunkenness so harmful?

2. What do reverence and self-control look like in today's culture?

3. Describe someone you know who demonstrated a radically different lifestyle after committing their life to Christ. What impact did this have on others?

FIVE

Sex, Marriage, and Faithfulness to the Lord

1 Corinthians 7:1–7 ESV *Now concerning the matters about which you wrote: "It is good for a man not to have sexual relations with a woman." ²But because of the temptation to sexual immorality, each man should have his own wife and each woman her own husband. ³The husband should give to his wife her conjugal rights, and likewise the wife to her husband. ⁴For the wife does not have authority over her own body, but the husband does. Likewise the husband does not have authority over his own body, but the wife does. ⁵Do not deprive one another, except perhaps by agreement for a limited time, that you may devote yourselves to prayer; but then come together again, so that Satan may not tempt you because of your lack of self-control.*

⁶Now as a concession, not a command, I say this. ⁷I wish that all were as I myself am. But each has his own gift from God, one of one kind and one of another.

Read also all of 1 Corinthians 7.

Key Observation. Both celibate singleness and the physicality of marriage honor God.

Understanding the Word. In Paul's first letter to the Corinthians, he responds to issues the Corinthians asked him to address. Here he tackles the belief that married couples are more holy if they refrain from sex. Although Corinth has a reputation for rampant sexual immorality, some Christians have responded with an extreme form of asceticism (the spiritual discipline of self-denial). Paul recognizes the power of sexual temptation. Thus, he affirms that sexual relations between a husband and wife help to stave off external temptations. His instructions to husbands and wives in verses 3–4 are remarkable for their mutuality. Not only does a husband have authority over his wife's body, but also a wife has authority over her husband's body! Paul's default assumption is that husband and wife share their bodies with one another and enjoy sexual pleasure. In addressing the concerns of the ascetics, Paul concedes that there may be times when husbands and wives should focus on spiritual matters such as prayer. This separation, however, should be temporary. Marriage is by nature an embodied relationship.

Paul himself is single (vv. 7–8), although scholars have speculated that he may have been married previously and is now a widower. (Anyone rising through the ranks of Judaism as Paul had done when he was younger would have been expected to marry.) Paul makes it clear that choosing celibate singleness is a gift from God. Those who cannot remain celibate ought to marry so as not to fall into sexual sin (v. 9).

In much of this chapter, Paul encourages believers to remain in whatever condition they find themselves. The ascetic group in Corinth is encouraging those who are married to divorce in order to be celibate. Paul disagrees. In verses 10–11, he addresses couples who have separated for ascetic reasons. They should be reconciled and the marriage covenant (including sexual relations) restored.

Paul shifts the discussion in verse 12 to those who have spouses who are not Christians. The ascetic concern for holiness has led some to think that an unbelieving spouse defiles the family. They seek to flee this unholiness through divorce. Again Paul urges Christians to stay committed to the marriage covenant. He argues that defilement does not spread to the believer, but rather the believer's holiness spreads to the rest of the family. This is not a promise that every unbeliever in the family will attain salvation. Rather, Paul suggests that the good character of a Christian provides testimony to other family members. This provides opportunity for them to come to know Christ. The believer should not leave such a marriage. But Paul recognizes that it may be impossible to keep an unbeliever from leaving; in such a case, believers are no longer held to the marriage covenant.

Although Paul affirms marriage, he also recognizes that family concerns can divide a person's attention (vv. 32–35). Someone who is able to live the single celibate life can focus all their energies on serving the Lord. Thus, Paul also affirms singleness as a means of devotion to God.

1. What should mutual authority over one's body look like in a marriage?

2. Why does misplaced sexuality dishonor God?

3. How can churches today affirm and aid those who are single?

WEEK SIX

GATHERING DISCUSSION OUTLINE

A. **Open session in prayer.** Ask that God would astonish us anew with fresh insight from God's Word and transform us into the disciples that Jesus desires us to become.

B. **View video for this week's readings.**

C. **What were key insights or takeaways that you gained from your reading during the week and from watching the video commentary?** In particular, how did these help you to grow in your faith and understanding of Scripture this week? What parts of the Bible lessons or study raised questions for you?

D. **Discuss selected questions from the daily readings.** Invite class members to share key insights or to raise questions that they found to be the most meaningful.

1. **KEY OBSERVATION:** Christ is the source of love that empowers us to submit to one another.

   DISCUSSION QUESTION: What are the best examples of mutual submission that you have seen?

2. **KEY OBSERVATION:** Paul asks husbands and wives to act as any believer should—with gentleness, humility, patience, peace, and sacrificial love.

   DISCUSSION QUESTION: Consider the similarities between the fruit of the Spirit (see Galatians 5:22–23) and the characteristics found here in Ephesians. How would marriages look different if these commands were fully lived out?

3. **KEY OBSERVATION:** Tension often exists between loyalty to Christ and loyalty to cultural expectations.

   DISCUSSION QUESTION: How does Christlike behavior help to diffuse tensions with the surrounding culture?

4. **KEY OBSERVATION:** Living reverently involves recognizing that you are in God's presence and your life belongs to God.

   DISCUSSION QUESTION: What do reverence and self-control look like in today's culture?

5. **KEY OBSERVATION:** Both celibate singleness and the physicality of marriage honor God.

   DISCUSSION QUESTION: Why does misplaced sexuality dishonor God?

E. **As the study concludes, consider specific ways that this week's Bible lessons invite you to grow and call you to change.** How do they call us to think differently? How do they challenge us to change in order to align ourselves with God's work in the world? What specific actions should we take to apply the insights of the lessons into our daily lives? What kind of person do our Bible lessons call us to become?

F. **Close session with prayer.** Emphasize God's ongoing work of transformation in our lives in preparation for loving mission and service in the world. Pray for absent class members as well as for persons whom we need to invite to join our study.

WEEK SEVEN

Negative Examples

ONE

Herodias and Her Daughter

Mark 6:17–26 NIV *For Herod himself had given orders to have John arrested, and he had him bound and put in prison. He did this because of Herodias, his brother Philip's wife, whom he had married. ¹⁸For John had been saying to Herod, "It is not lawful for you to have your brother's wife." ¹⁹So Herodias nursed a grudge against John and wanted to kill him. But she was not able to, ²⁰because Herod feared John and protected him, knowing him to be a righteous and holy man. When Herod heard John, he was greatly puzzled; yet he liked to listen to him.*

²¹Finally the opportune time came. On his birthday Herod gave a banquet for his high officials and military commanders and the leading men of Galilee. ²²When the daughter of Herodias came in and danced, she pleased Herod and his dinner guests.

The king said to the girl, "Ask me for anything you want, and I'll give it to you." ²³And he promised her with an oath, "Whatever you ask I will give you, up to half my kingdom."

²⁴She went out and said to her mother, "What shall I ask for?"

"The head of John the Baptist," she answered.

²⁵At once the girl hurried in to the king with the request: "I want you to give me right now the head of John the Baptist on a platter."

²⁶The king was greatly distressed, but because of his oaths and his dinner guests, he did not want to refuse her.

Read also Mark 6:27–29; Matthew 14:1–12; and Luke 3:19–20.

Key Observation. Self-centered thinking often leads to violence and destruction.

Understanding the Word. This week we will explore stories describing women who serve their own interests rather than those of the kingdom of God. These stories provide a strong contrast with the examples of godly women we have recently discussed.

Our first story involves two women in the Herod dynasty, a family tree that sounds like a modern soap opera. Herod Antipas, one of several sons of Herod the Great, ruled over Galilee during the ministry of Jesus. Herod's half brother, Philip, married Herodias. Later they divorced so Herodias could marry Herod (who was also her half uncle). John the Baptist openly condemns the incestuous marriage (see Leviticus 18:16 and 20:21). Herodias resents this judgment and seeks a chance to get rid of John.

The Gospels record that Herod has a fickle attitude toward John. He resents John's public outcry against his marriage. But Herod also fears the power of this popular preacher and the crowds that accompany him. He likes to listen to John, but finds him confusing.

Herodias, however, will not lay aside her anger with John for publicly calling her a sinner. She uses the occasion of Herod's birthday party to manipulate Herod into getting rid of John. Key leaders from the region attend, and Herod feels compelled to show them a good time. His stepdaughter dances for the men, and Herod is very pleased with her performance. (The text doesn't say whether this is an erotic dance. If so, it only confirms John's accusations about Herod's incestuous nature.) Herod tells his stepdaughter he will give her anything she wants, and uses a proverbial expression ("up to half my kingdom") to emphasize his generosity. The girl defers to her mother's wishes and asks for John's head on a platter.

Herod finds himself in a bind. He doesn't want to kill John, but he has publicly proclaimed he will do anything for his stepdaughter. If he goes back on his promise, he will lose honor among a room full of powerful people. Herod chooses his own interests over the life of an innocent man. Among all the platters of food and wine at the party, John's still-warm head is openly displayed.

This tale of revenge and manipulation strongly differs from biblical descriptions of faithful women:

- Herodias is a social climber, willing to divorce one brother so she can marry the more powerful brother. But a Christian woman remains loyal to her marriage vows.

- Herodias rejects and resents the call to repentance, seeking revenge instead. But a Christian woman learns in submission and gentleness of spirit.

- Herodias uses her daughter to manipulate a weak-willed husband into murdering her enemy. A Christian woman submits to her husband, just as her husband mutually submits through love and tender care.

- Herodias displays the bloody trophy of her victim as a warning not to antagonize her. But a Christian woman lives such a godly life that no one will have a negative word to speak against her.

These contrasting values clearly depict the otherworldly nature of the Christian life.

1. Which of the actions of Herodias do you find most shocking and why?

2. Which part of the gospel message today meets with the most resistance?

3. Why do people often choose hatred and revenge over kindness and love?

TWO

The Slave Girl in Philippi

Acts 16:16–18 *One day, as we were going to the place of prayer, we met a slave-girl who had a spirit of divination and brought her owners a great deal of money by fortune-telling. ¹⁷While she followed Paul and us, she would cry out, "These men are slaves of the Most High God, who proclaim to you a way of salvation." ¹⁸She kept doing this for many days. But Paul, very much annoyed, turned and said to the spirit, "I order you in the name of Jesus Christ to come out of her." And it came out that very hour.*

Key Observation. Not everyone who speaks a kernel of truth is on your side.

Understanding the Word. The slave girl in this story has no name and no will of her own. We don't know her background, other than the fact that she is enslaved both physically and spiritually. The specific spirit that afflicts her allows her to tell fortunes. Her owners take advantage of her condition to make money from her fortune-telling. She does the work, and they get the money.

The phrase used for "spirit of divination" translates literally as the "spirit of the python." It was a common phrase used for those with spirits of divination, but the source is Greek mythology. The Greeks believed that the god Apollo killed a huge snake at Delphi. A temple was built in Apollo's honor at Delphi, where a priestess told the future. Called the "oracle at Delphi," she sat on a chair over a large crack in the earth. Legend tells of vapors rising through the crack and inspiring her divine prophecies. The oracle at Delphi was considered the most powerful prophetess in the Greco-Roman world. Having a "spirit of the python," then, would imply that a strong spirit connected to Apollo controlled the girl. The fact that the slave girl in Philippi makes "a great deal of money" for her owners through fortune-telling confirms that the people believe she is powerful.

Then along comes Paul. Just as the demons in the Gospels cried out that Jesus was the Son of God, so, too, here the demonic spirit declares that Paul and his companions serve the Most High God. They are proclaiming "a way of salvation." (The Greeks in the crowd would hear this as *a* way among many, while the Christians would hear this as *the* way of salvation.) This slave girl continues to follow them and cry out these words for several days. Although she is proclaiming truth about Paul, her incessant loud cries are interrupting and disturbing the work he is trying to accomplish. With a single sentence invoking the name of Jesus, Paul is able to cast out the spirit. The Greco-Roman onlookers would be shocked that the spirit of the python could be so easily defeated.

The slave girl fades from the story and we never learn what happens to her after she loses her moneymaking powers. But her spiritual freedom comes at a high price for Paul and Silas: the slave owners are so angry at losing their future profits that they drag the pair into the marketplace. Paul and Silas are beaten and thrown in jail.

1. In what ways do people sometimes misuse truth to hurt rather than to help? How should you respond when this happens?

2. Why is there often a high price for preaching the gospel?

3. In what ways do you need to be reminded that the power of Christ is greater than worldly powers?

THREE

The Mother of the Sons of Zebedee

Matthew 20:20–23 *Then the mother of the sons of Zebedee came to him with her sons, and kneeling before him, she asked a favor of him. *[21]*And he said to her, "What do you want?" She said to him, "Declare that these two sons of mine will sit, one at your right hand and one at your left, in your kingdom." *[22]*But Jesus answered, "You do not know what you are asking. Are you able to drink the cup that I am about to drink?" They said to him, "We are able." *[23]*He said to them, "You will indeed drink my cup, but to sit at my right hand and at my left, this is not mine to grant, but it is for those for whom it has been prepared by my Father."*

Key Observation. Ambition can blind us to God's greater plan.

Understanding the Word. James and John, the sons of Zebedee, were among the first disciples of Jesus. They had worked as fishermen for their family business, which was successful enough to need hired men (see Mark 1:20). Their bold personalities had earned them the nickname of "Sons of Thunder" (Mark 3:17). The forthright zeal of James and John appears in Luke 9:54, where they ask Jesus if they should call down fire upon the Samaritans who rejected Jesus. (Jesus, of course, rebukes them.)

It appears that the apple does not fall far from the tree. Their mother is just as bold as they are. Jesus has already told the twelve disciples that they will reign with him on twelve thrones, judging the tribes of Israel (see Matthew 19:28). But for the mother of James and John, this promise is not enough. She wants to make sure that her boys receive the highest positions of honor among the disciples. After all, Peter, James, and John comprise Jesus' inner circle, his best friends among the Twelve. She is only ensuring that her sons get what they deserve for their hard work and devotion. They left their fishing business in order to become itinerant preachers, despised by the religious elite and suspected of dissension by Roman officials. She wants to make sure that her sons will have a legacy. And what a legacy she wants for them! Sitting at the right hand of a ruler was *the* place of honor; sitting at the left hand was the next best position. She will boldly ask for the best for her sons. In order to sway Jesus, the mother approaches him with great deference and respect, kneeling down before him.

It is clear from Jesus' response, however, that he shrewdly recognizes the family dynamics involved. This is not her request alone; her sons have put her up to it. (In Mark 10:35–40, the brothers ask Jesus directly; their mother is not even mentioned.) Here in Matthew, Jesus responds with the plural "you." That is, the three of you do not understand the implications of your request. Prior to this discussion, Jesus had predicted his suffering and death (see Matthew 20:17–19). When he asks them now if they can bear this cup, they have already forgotten the earlier conversation. Jesus is referring to suffering and judgment. When the sons proclaim their steadfast loyalty, Jesus finally agrees that they will drink the cup. They still miss his meaning, but they will later understand. The disciples will face persecution and James will be martyred under Herod Agrippa I (see Acts 12:1–2). Ultimately, though, Jesus makes it clear that his Father in heaven has already made decisions about honor in the afterlife. Jesus will not overturn his Father's plans. The humility that Jesus shows counters the audacity of his disciples and their mother. The family of Zebedee has yet to learn that the path to glory lies along the road of self-sacrifice.

1. When does defending someone's accomplishments turn into inappropriate pride or bias?

2. How can believers keep from turning bitter when we don't get what we think we deserve?

3. How can we ambitiously serve the kingdom without falling into worldly desires for recognition?

FOUR

The Widows Who Live for Pleasure

1 Timothy 5:3–6, 9–16 ESV *Honor widows who are truly widows. ⁴But if a widow has children or grandchildren, let them first learn to show godliness to their own household and to make some return to their parents, for this is pleasing in the sight of God. ⁵She who is truly a widow, left all alone, has set her hope on God and continues in supplications and prayers night and day, ⁶but she who is self-indulgent is dead even while she lives. . . .*

⁹Let a widow be enrolled if she is not less than sixty years of age, having been the wife of one husband, ¹⁰and having a reputation for good works: if she has brought up children, has shown hospitality, has washed the feet of the saints, has cared for the afflicted, and has devoted herself to every good work. ¹¹But refuse to enroll younger widows, for when their passions draw them away from Christ, they desire to marry ¹²and so incur condemnation for having abandoned their former faith. ¹³Besides that, they learn to be idlers, going about from house to house, and not only idlers, but also gossips and busybodies, saying what they should not. ¹⁴So I would have younger widows marry, bear children, manage their households, and give the adversary no occasion for slander. ¹⁵For some have already strayed after Satan. ¹⁶If any believing woman has relatives who are widows, let her care for them. Let the church not be burdened, so that it may care for those who are truly widows.

Key Observation. Discernment is necessary when helping others.

Understanding the Word. This section of the letter to Timothy distinguishes between those women who are truly widows in need of the help of the church and those widows who should not receive aid. Some widows were wealthy, but many found themselves destitute after their husbands had died. There was no social security system in the ancient world; widows could find themselves in a dire position if they had no sons or fathers to provide for them. As a result, God commanded his people to show special care to widows (e.g., Exodus 22:22; Deuteronomy 24:17; Isaiah 1:17).

Nonetheless, some of the widows in Ephesus have chased after worldly desires and have abandoned the faith. The letter contrasts true widows with those who are "self-indulgent," a phrase used elsewhere to describe the sins of Sodom (see Ezekiel 16:49) and rich oppressors (see James 5:5). In those passages, the self-indulgent refuse to help the needy and do not treat them justly. God pronounces judgment against such wanton excess. In 1 Timothy 5:6, the self-indulgent widow is "dead even while she lives." She seeks life in worldly pleasures and yet fails to realize she has found only spiritual death.

A concern also surrounds the younger widows. Their sexual passions make them want to remarry, and this, in turn, leads them away from their commitment to Christ. This does not mean that marriage is a sin. In fact, verse 14 urges younger widows to remarry! Rather, verse 11 refers to women who let their passions control them. They are pursuing marriage so fervently that they become distracted and lose their devotion to Christ. In chasing after romantic love, they reject their first love: Christ. Once they have lost their anchor in the faith, they turn to other destructive habits as well. These include a lack of work ethic, a desire to gossip, and a tendency to meddle in the business of others. Such activities lead one closer to Satan than to Christ (v. 15).

The advice to Timothy, then, is to make sure that those women who are enrolled on the church's list of widows are older women who have no family to care for them. (Verses 8 and 16 command believers to care for family members who are widows.) This list may have been a record of those who needed provision and care. In later centuries, however, an order of widows developed that was responsible for prayer, teaching younger women, and hospitality. It is uncertain whether this order had developed as early as the first century. Younger widows, however, are instructed to marry, to work hard to raise their children, and to become good household managers. Laziness and gossip have no part in the Christian life. The godly woman who gives no cause for reproach is the woman who hopes in God, prays regularly, and has devoted herself to every good work.

1. In what ways can self-indulgence and seeking after romantic love lead one away from Christ?

2. Why are laziness, gossip, and meddling so destructive?

3. Why shouldn't we aid everyone who asks for help? How can we balance generosity and wisdom?

FIVE

Sapphira

Acts 5:1–5a, 7–10 NIV *Now a man named Ananias, together with his wife Sapphira, also sold a piece of property. ²With his wife's full knowledge he kept back part of the money for himself, but brought the rest and put it at the apostles' feet.*

³Then Peter said, "Ananias, how is it that Satan has so filled your heart that you have lied to the Holy Spirit and have kept for yourself some of the money you received for the land? ⁴Didn't it belong to you before it was sold? And after it was sold, wasn't the money at your disposal? What made you think of doing such a thing? You have not lied just to human beings but to God."

⁵When Ananias heard this, he fell down and died. . . .

⁷About three hours later his wife came in, not knowing what had happened. ⁸Peter asked her, "Tell me, is this the price you and Ananias got for the land?"

"Yes," she said, "that is the price."

⁹Peter said to her, "How could you conspire to test the Spirit of the Lord? Listen! The feet of the men who buried your husband are at the door, and they will carry you out also."

¹⁰At that moment she fell down at his feet and died. Then the young men came in and, finding her dead, carried her out and buried her beside her husband.

Key Observation. A spouse's first obligation is to honor God, even if it means disagreeing with their partner.

Understanding the Word. This disturbing story occurs just as the early church is beginning to flourish. In 4:32–37, we learn that all the believers are of one heart and mind and share their possessions with anyone who has need. Barnabas (who will later travel with Paul) provides an example of this generosity: he sells a field and lays the proceeds at the feet of the apostles.

In contrast, Ananias and Sapphira demonstrate greed and deception through their sale of property. Despite the fact that they are not required to sell their property or share their wealth (5:4), they pretend to imitate Barnabas. Their pride makes them seek recognition from the church, and their greed leads them to hide part of the proceeds. They are falsifying the Holy Spirit. That is, they pretend to have the same fruit of the Spirit that others have demonstrated.

Peter confronts the husband first, accusing Ananias of allowing Satan to direct his choices rather than the Holy Spirit. The real sin, Peter says, is lying to God. When Ananias hears these convicting words, he falls down, dead. This shocking event demonstrates that during acute periods of God's revelation, God manifests his power and judgment more forcefully. In Joshua 7, for example, Joshua and the people of God began entering the promised land. Achan, however, "kept back" (in the original this is the same word as used in Acts 5:2 for Ananias and Sapphira) some of the bounty that should have been dedicated to the Lord. God's judgment resulted in death.

In Acts 5, judgment occurs against both Ananias and his wife, Sapphira. Not long after the body of Ananias has been carried out, Sapphira enters the room. The story emphasizes her mutual culpability for lying to God: she knows the real price of the property but lies to Peter when he asks her about it. She is a dutiful wife and supports her husband. But because she supports *the sin* of her husband, she, too, falls down dead after Peter proclaims the truth. She and her husband "conspire[d]" (literally, "agreed together") to test the Holy Spirit (v. 9). Their harmony in lying stands in stark contrast to the harmony of the church in 4:32. In testing the Spirit, Ananias and Sapphira have challenged God's authority. Their actions are an expression of disbelief and disobedience. They defy God, thinking God will not react. Just as the Israelites who tested God in the wilderness did not make it out of the desert, so, too, Ananias and Sapphira cannot escape the consequences of their lie.

We have explored many stories that demonstrate the mutuality of husband and wife. In the case of Ananias and Sapphira, they both equally share in God's judgment for their sin. Their story makes clear that Sapphira's first obligation should have been to honor God, even if that meant defying her husband.

1. Which sin do you think is more destructive: pride or greed? Why?

2. In what ways might you be tempted to pretend you have the same successes as others in your church?

3. What kinds of decisions might require a spouse to disagree with their partner in order to honor God?

WEEK SEVEN

GATHERING DISCUSSION OUTLINE

A. **Open session in prayer.** Ask that God would astonish us anew with fresh insight from God's Word and transform us into the disciples that Jesus desires us to become.

B. **View video for this week's readings.**

C. **What were key insights or takeaways that you gained from your reading during the week and from watching the video commentary?** In particular, how did these help you to grow in your faith and understanding of Scripture this week? What parts of the Bible lessons or study raised questions for you?

D. **Discuss selected questions from the daily readings.** Invite class members to share key insights or to raise questions that they found to be the most meaningful.

1. **KEY OBSERVATION:** Self-centered thinking often leads to violence and destruction.

    DISCUSSION QUESTION: Why do people often choose hatred and revenge over kindness and love?

2. **KEY OBSERVATION:** Not everyone who speaks a kernel of truth is on your side.

    DISCUSSION QUESTION: In what ways do people sometimes misuse truth to hurt rather than to help? How should you respond when this happens?

3. **KEY OBSERVATION:** Ambition can blind us to God's greater plan.

   DISCUSSION QUESTION: How can we ambitiously serve the kingdom without falling into worldly desires for recognition?

4. **KEY OBSERVATION:** Discernment is necessary when helping others.

   DISCUSSION QUESTION: Why shouldn't we aid everyone who asks for help? How can we balance generosity and wisdom?

5. **KEY OBSERVATION:** A spouse's first obligation is to honor God, even if it means disagreeing with their partner.

   DISCUSSION QUESTION: What kinds of decisions might require a spouse to disagree with their partner in order to honor God?

E. **As the study concludes, consider specific ways that this week's Bible lessons invite you to grow and call you to change.** How do they call us to think differently? How do they challenge us to change in order to align ourselves with God's work in the world? What specific actions should we take to apply the insights of the lessons into our daily lives? What kind of person do our Bible lessons call us to become?

F. **Close session with prayer.** Emphasize God's ongoing work of transformation in our lives in preparation for loving mission and service in the world. Pray for absent class members as well as for persons whom we need to invite to join our study.

WEEK EIGHT

Trajectories of Restoration

ONE

Female Prophets in the New Age

Acts 2:16–18 NIV *No, this is what was spoken by the prophet Joel:*
[17]"In the last days, God says, I will pour out my Spirit on all people. Your sons and daughters will prophesy, your young men will see visions, your old men will dream dreams. [18]Even on my servants, both men and women, I will pour out my Spirit in those days, and they will prophesy."

Acts 21:8–9 NIV *Leaving the next day, we reached Caesarea and stayed at the house of Philip the evangelist, one of the Seven. [9]He had four unmarried daughters who prophesied.*

Key Observation. The Holy Spirit is for all believers.

Understanding the Word. This week we will explore various ways that the work of God in the early church demonstrated the beginning of the new creation and the overturning of worldly hierarchies.

Our first story explores the fulfillment of Old Testament prophecy in the fledgling church. The beginning of Acts records the birth of the church during the Jewish Pentecost festival. Believers—both men and women (1:14)—gather in Jerusalem (2:1). The Holy Spirit fills the house and rests upon each person. This enables them to preach the gospel in foreign languages. Others nearby hear the sound of a violent wind and question what has happened. Some sneer at the believers and claim their different speech is the result of drunkenness. The apostle Peter, however, responds that God has sent the Holy Spirit in fulfillment of Scripture. Jesus died and has been raised, and now the last days have begun.

The first scripture Peter cites to support his theological argument is Joel 2:28–29. The prophet Joel had predicted a time when God would pour forth his spirit on all people, regardless of age, gender, or social status. Peter adds to Joel's prophecy in verse 29 the line, "and they will prophesy" (Acts 2:18). Peter's point is that when God works in the last days to restore all things, the hierarchical structures of this world will no longer matter. God's blessings are for all his people.

Luke himself makes this evident when he writes his Gospel and Acts. Luke is well known for pairing male and female characters together. At the birth of Jesus, both Simeon and Anna prophesy over the child. By the end of Luke's second book, he wants readers to remember that the Holy Spirit is for all people. Thus, he includes a reference to Philip's four unmarried daughters who prophesy.

Philip first appeared in chapter 6. Philip was one of seven men chosen to distribute food to widows after a dispute had broken out among believers. The seven men were "full of the Spirit and of wisdom" (6:3). After Stephen died and Saul began persecuting the church, Philip went to Samaria and preached the gospel, bringing many to faith (8:4–13). Later Philip explained Scripture to the Ethiopian eunuch. Afterward, the Spirit carried Philip away to Azotus (8:26–40). Eventually he returned to his home in Caesarea.

When Luke mentions Philip again in Acts 21:8, Philip is offering hospitality to Paul, who years earlier had caused Philip and others to flee Jerusalem! While Paul and his companions stay at Philip's house, another prophet arrives and predicts that Paul will be jailed in Jerusalem (21:10–11).

Luke mentions the four daughters of Philip in the midst of Paul's visit. They are unmarried and all four prophesy. They have seen the Holy Spirit at work repeatedly in their father. They have witnessed the transformation of Paul from persecutor to church planter. And they now participate with others in prophesying God's word to the church. These young women stand as living testimony that the words of Joel have come to fruition.

1. Peter's understanding of events was shaped by his understanding of Scripture. In what ways has Scripture shaped your understanding of the events in your own life?

2. In what ways do you hope that the kingdom of God will overturn the hierarchies in this world?

3. Where do you see the Holy Spirit crossing boundaries (young/old, male/female, rich/poor, etc.) in your own church?

TWO

Qualifications for Leaders in the Church

1 Timothy 3:8–13 *Deacons likewise must be serious, not double-tongued, not indulging in much wine, not greedy for money;* ⁹*they must hold fast to the mystery of the faith with a clear conscience.* ¹⁰*And let them first be tested; then, if they prove themselves blameless, let them serve as deacons.* ¹¹*Women likewise must be serious, not slanderers, but temperate, faithful in all things.* ¹²*Let deacons be married only once, and let them manage their children and their households well;* ¹³*for those who serve well as deacons gain a good standing for themselves and great boldness in the faith that is in Christ Jesus.*

Key Observation. Personal integrity is a key qualification for leadership in the church.

Understanding the Word. In this section, Timothy receives instructions regarding qualifications for leaders. Although today we might ask potential leaders for résumés listing previous work experience, the early church was more concerned with personal integrity. Living the faith was a key requirement for leading those of faith.

The first seven verses of chapter 3 describe requirements for overseers ("bishops"). These verses do not distinguish between male and female overseers. Many English translations refer to male overseers, but in the Greek masculine terms are used even when a group includes both men and women. Unless the text explicitly excludes women, we can assume both genders are being addressed.

The next section addresses deacons, although the role of the deacon is not clearly defined. The word itself means "servant." Paul uses it of himself and his coworkers and in Acts it refers to disciples who administered supplies for needy widows. The term may refer loosely to those in the church who lead through various acts of service.

The section begins by stating that deacons must be "serious" (or "respectable," the same word used for female deacons in verse 11), sincere, not tempted to drunkenness, and not greedy. They must hold fast to the deep teaching of the faith and be blameless. The letter then specifically addresses female deacons in verse 11. The word used here can mean either "wives" or "women." Some interpreters have suggested that the letter is referring to the behavior required for wives of deacons. The wording, however, does not say "their" wives as one would expect if "wives" were intended. Instead, it says "women likewise." This implies that the office and expectations are the same even when the gender is not. It would also be odd to list behavior for deacons' wives but not for elders' wives. Instead, verse 11 provides behavioral expectations that apply specifically to female deacons. The requirements are very similar to those for male deacons. Female deacons must be "serious, not slanderers, but temperate, faithful in all things." Given the false teaching that was prevalent among women in Ephesus, this additional exhortation is not surprising. When women are providing service to the church, they must not be like the gossiping widows (5:13) or authority-grasping false teachers (2:12) who are reprimanded elsewhere in the letter.

In 3:12, the instructions now refer to all deacons, regardless of gender. The phrase "be married only once" (literally, "one-woman man") is an idiom that means faithfulness in marriage. Some interpreters have taken the literal expression to mean that deacons must be male and married. If the phrase were taken literally, however, then single or widowed believers (like Paul) would be excluded. The phrase simply requires deacons to be monogamous in marriage.

The final requirement that deacons be good managers of their households (v. 12) is similar to the command to young widows in 5:14. Household management is a responsibility of both men and women.

The whole section wraps up in verse 13 with a word of encouragement: deacons—both men and women—who serve well will receive good standing and boldness in the faith.

1. On what basis are leaders in your own church normally chosen?

2. What does respectability (or seriousness) look like in today's culture?

3. Why is personal integrity so important for leadership?

THREE

Daughters of God, the Temple of God

2 Corinthians 6:14–7:1 ESV *Do not be unequally yoked with unbelievers. For what partnership has righteousness with lawlessness? Or what fellowship has light with darkness?* *¹⁵What accord has Christ with Belial? Or what portion does a believer share with an unbeliever?* *¹⁶What agreement has the temple of God with idols? For we are the temple of the living God; as God said,*

"I will make my dwelling among them and walk among them, and I will be their God, and they shall be my people. *¹⁷Therefore go out from their midst, and be separate from them, says the Lord, and touch no unclean thing; then I will welcome you,* *¹⁸and I will be a father to you, and you shall be sons and daughters to me, says the Lord Almighty."*

⁷:¹Since we have these promises, beloved, let us cleanse ourselves from every defilement of body and spirit, bringing holiness to completion in the fear of God.

Key Observation. God's plan of salvation includes women in a way that transcends cultural boundaries.

Understanding the Word. In this passage, Paul urges believers to separate from unbelievers. Elsewhere, Paul has confronted the Corinthians because they have listened to competing teachers. He urges them to return to a true understanding of the gospel. Some interpreters suggest that 6:14–7:1 doesn't match his argument and is a later, non-Pauline, addition to the letter. However, the passage fits because it highlights the consequences that will result if the Corinthians continue to reject Paul: they will yoke themselves to those who do not believe the gospel. In order to prevent this, Paul urges the Corinthians to separate themselves from those unbelievers.

Paul asks a series of rhetorical questions to contrast God with the unrighteousness of the world. In a city filled with temples and idols, Paul reminds the Corinthians that they, metaphorically, are God's temple. The term Paul uses refers to the sacred inner sanctuary. If God lives in them, then they must not associate with false teachers or live unholy lifestyles.

In verse 16, Paul cites several scriptures to remind the Corinthians that God has promised to live with his people (see Leviticus 26:11–12; Jeremiah 32:38;

Ezekiel 37:27). Then Paul argues in verse 17 that the people must be holy if God is to live among them (see Isaiah 52:11; Ezekiel 20:34, 41). Finally, Paul proclaims that God has established a new family relationship with his people. God is their Father and they are his sons and daughters. The scripture comes from 2 Samuel 7:14, where God promises David an eternal inheritance. Paul now applies it to the people of God and intentionally changes the language to include women. "He shall be a son to me" becomes "You shall be sons and daughters to me." (This may recall Isaiah 43:6, in which God restores his sons *and* daughters.) Paul recognizes that the covenant promises of God include both men and women and they are now fulfilled through Christ. Some church leaders today have questioned whether Scripture should be changed to create gender-inclusive language. Already in the first century, however, the apostle Paul saw the importance of creating a gender-inclusive translation.

Paul's language is even more remarkable because it portrays women as part of the new temple of God (v. 16). When Paul writes, the Jerusalem temple is still standing. Women are allowed only in the outer courts, not the inner sanctuary. Their menstrual cycle makes them impure, and Levitical regulations require cleansing rituals. But Paul declares that Christ has inaugurated a new age. Now the true sanctuary is comprised of believing men *and women*. The holiness of women is no longer defined by biological processes, but by Christ living in them. When Paul refers to "defilement of body and spirit" in 7:1, he is not thinking of ritual uncleanness. Although Paul writes to a primarily Gentile audience, the Jewish members of the Corinthian church would recognize these powerful implications. True holiness has nothing to do with gender and everything to do with living as a new creation in Christ (5:17).

1. How might a first-century woman have responded to the idea that she is a temple for God?

2. How does gender-inclusive language change the way a person perceives the promises of God?

3. What cultural boundaries still need to be crossed to fully embrace women in the kingdom of God? How can your church work toward this goal?

FOUR

Female Coworkers and House Church Leaders

Acts 16:13–15, 40 *On the sabbath day we went outside the gate by the river, where we supposed there was a place of prayer; and we sat down and spoke to the women who had gathered there. ¹⁴A certain woman named Lydia, a worshiper of God, was listening to us; she was from the city of Thyatira and a dealer in purple cloth. The Lord opened her heart to listen eagerly to what was said by Paul. ¹⁵When she and her household were baptized, she urged us, saying, "If you have judged me to be faithful to the Lord, come and stay at my home." And she prevailed upon us. . . .*

⁴⁰After leaving the prison they went to Lydia's home; and when they had seen and encouraged the brothers and sisters there, they departed.

2 John 1–2, 4–5, 13 ESV *The elder to the elect lady and her children, whom I love in truth, and not only I, but also all who know the truth, ²because of the truth that abides in us and will be with us forever. . . .*

⁴I rejoiced greatly to find some of your children walking in the truth, just as we were commanded by the Father. ⁵And now I ask you, dear lady—not as though I were writing you a new commandment, but the one we have had from the beginning—that we love one another. . . .

¹³The children of your elect sister greet you.

Read also Philippians 4:2–3; Colossians 4:15; and Romans 16:6, 12.

Key Observation. Women were actively involved in leadership in many of the early churches.

Understanding the Word. Today's passages demonstrate the variety of women not only involved in the early churches, but also actively leading within them. In Philippi, one of the first people to whom Paul preaches the gospel is Lydia, a dealer in purple cloth. This is a luxury item and indicates that Lydia is a wealthy merchant. In both Acts 16:15 and 16:40, Luke refers to the home in which Paul stays as Lydia's home, not her husband's. In the

Greco-Roman world, a home was usually referred to by the name of the male head of household. Thus, it is likely that Lydia is widowed and is the head of her own household. This wealthy, independent woman believes in Christ and offers hospitality to Paul and his companions. It appears that the newly converted Philippians begin meeting in Lydia's home, since Paul "encouraged the brothers and sisters there" (16:40).

But Lydia is not the only woman in Philippi whose service merits mention. When Paul writes to the Philippians from prison, he specifically urges Euodia and Syntyche to set aside their differences and be unified. In his address, however, Paul states that these women "have contended at my side in the cause of the gospel" (Phil. 4:3 NIV) with the rest of his coworkers. That is, Paul places them at the same level as his male colleagues who helped to spread the gospel message.

In Colossians 4:15, we hear about Nympha, who hosts a church in her house in Laodicea. Thus, she too, is likely a wealthy widow who offers hospitality and leadership.

Similarly, in Romans 16, Paul declares that Mary (v. 6), Tryphaena and Tryphosa (who likely are sisters), and Persis (v. 12) have all worked hard in the Lord. Paul regularly uses the idea of "working" in the Lord to refer to those who preach the gospel and serve the church in various ways. Paul refers to his own missionary activity as "work" in the Lord in 1 Corinthians 15:10 and "labor" in Philippians 2:16. He describes others who "work" for the gospel in 1 Thessalonians 5:12 (NIV). There is no reason to think he uses the term differently for these faithful women.

Finally, John's second letter is addressed to "the elect lady and her children" (v. 1). Many modern scholars have taken this reference as metaphorical, referring to a church and its members. Although female metaphors for the church (such as "bride of Christ") do occur in the New Testament, nowhere is the church referred to as a "lady." Rather, it is likely that John writes the letter to a female church leader and her metaphorical children (that is, the members of her house church). This would be consistent with both 1 and 3 John, where John addresses church members as "children." Thus, when John sends greetings from the "children" of the lady's "sister" (2 John 13), he is likely referring to greetings sent from members of another house church led by yet another woman.

Unfortunately, the work of many of these female church leaders has been obscured over time. But the prevalence of these female leaders in the earliest churches demonstrates the inauguration of the kingdom of God.

1. Which of these leaders is most surprising to you? Why?

2. What activities does Paul likely have in mind when he refers to "workers" for the gospel?

3. How have you seen women in the churches today working for the gospel?

FIVE

Neither Male nor Female

Galatians 3:26–29 ESV *for in Christ Jesus you are all sons of God, through faith. ²⁷For as many of you as were baptized into Christ have put on Christ. ²⁸There is neither Jew nor Greek, there is neither slave nor free, there is no male and female, for you are all one in Christ Jesus. ²⁹And if you are Christ's, then you are Abraham's offspring, heirs according to promise.*

Key Observation. Everyone who lives in Christ is an heir to the kingdom of God.

Understanding the Word. When Paul writes to the Galatians, he is upset. After he had left Galatia to start other churches, certain Jewish Christians came into Galatia and told the Gentile Christians that they had to follow all the laws of the Torah if they were going to receive salvation. Paul writes this letter to help the Gentile Christians understand that it is only by faith in Jesus that anyone is saved. Even Jews receive salvation by believing in Jesus, not by following Torah.

Since there is only one means of salvation—faith—*anyone* who believes belongs to the one people of God. Paul emphasizes the unity of all who are "in Christ" (v. 26). That is, through the power of the Holy Spirit, believers immerse themselves in the life of Christ and are being transformed into Christ's likeness. Jesus has inaugurated the new age, and those who are "in" him now experience a new reality. The typical divisions of the world—culture, socio-economic status, and gender—no longer have the last word.

Paul starts with the key division he has been addressing in this letter: Jew and Gentile. Jews took pride in being the elect people of God and the Romans took pride in being the dominant political and cultural power of the day. But Paul says that cultural and ethnic distinctions do not matter to God, who has made salvation available to all people in Christ.

The second division—slave or free—was a key status marker in the Greco-Roman world. Slaves were on the lowest rung of the societal ladder. They had no legal rights and could not inherit property. But Paul declares that this identity marker no longer matters. Economic status means nothing to God.

The final division Paul highlights is male and female. In the Greco-Roman world, men were considered superior to women in intellect, strength, and emotional fortitude. The male head of household was the final authority. In Jewish homes, women could not initiate divorce or inherit property (as a general rule). Although Roman laws allowed women to divorce and inherit property, a male relative still had control over the woman's property. Paul's declaration that there is no longer male and female overturns gender as a marker of status and power. The only identity marker that matters to God is faith in Christ.

Imagine the shock of Christian slaves and women when they hear that they now have the status of "sons" of God (v. 26). In God's kingdom, they are no longer under the control of a male head of household. In God's kingdom, they are no longer treated as property. Now, like the men who previously ruled over them, they are "offspring" who inherit the kingdom (v. 29). Their identity has been radically redefined in Christ.

1. What are the most important status markers in today's society?

2. How does being "in Christ" radically redefine our identities?

3. God's kingdom levels the playing field: those without power in society are lifted up, while those in power must relinquish power. How is God calling you to level the playing field in your relationships with other believers?

WEEK EIGHT

GATHERING DISCUSSION OUTLINE

A. Open session in prayer. Ask that God would astonish us anew with fresh insight from God's Word and transform us into the disciples that Jesus desires us to become.

B. View video for this week's readings.

C. What were key insights or takeaways that you gained from your reading during the week and from watching the video commentary? In particular, how did these help you to grow in your faith and understanding of Scripture this week? What parts of the Bible lessons or study raised questions for you?

D. Discuss selected questions from the daily readings. Invite class members to share key insights or to raise questions that they found to be the most meaningful.

1. **KEY OBSERVATION:** The Holy Spirit is for all believers.

    DISCUSSION QUESTION: Where do you see the Holy Spirit crossing boundaries (young/old, male/female, rich/poor, etc.) in your own church?

2. **KEY OBSERVATION:** Personal integrity is a key qualification for leadership in the church.

    DISCUSSION QUESTION: Why is personal integrity so important for leadership?

3. **KEY OBSERVATION:** God's plan of salvation includes women in a way that transcends cultural boundaries.

   DISCUSSION QUESTION: What cultural boundaries still need to be crossed to fully embrace women in the kingdom of God? How can your church work toward this goal?

4. **KEY OBSERVATION:** Women were actively involved in leadership in many of the early churches.

   DISCUSSION QUESTION: How have you seen women in the churches today working for the gospel?

5. **KEY OBSERVATION:** Everyone who lives in Christ is an heir to the kingdom of God.

   DISCUSSION QUESTION: God's kingdom levels the playing field: those without power in society are lifted up, while those in power must relinquish power. How is God calling you to level the playing field in your relationships with other believers?

E. **As the study concludes, consider specific ways that this week's Bible lessons invite you to grow and call you to change.** How do they call us to think differently? How do they challenge us to change in order to align ourselves with God's work in the world? What specific actions should we take to apply the insights of the lessons into our daily lives? What kind of person do our Bible lessons call us to become?

F. **Close session with prayer.** Emphasize God's ongoing work of transformation in our lives in preparation for loving mission and service in the world.

CPSIA information can be obtained
at www.ICGtesting.com
Printed in the USA
LVHW050758280623
750323LV00005B/18